The Arab Moslems in the United States

The Arab Moslems in the United States

Religion and Assimilation

By

Abdo A. Elkholy

Northern Illinois University

COLLEGE & UNIVERSITY PRESS · *Publishers*

NEW HAVEN, CONN.

Library of Congress Catalog Card Number: 66-28603

MANUFACTURED IN THE UNITED STATES OF AMERICA BY
UNITED PRINTING SERVICES, INC.
NEW HAVEN, CONNECTICUT

For my teachers
Muhammad El-Bahay and Morroe Berger

Preface

During the summer of 1961, while Egypt was celebrating the ninth anniversary of its Revolution, the Federation of Islamic Associations in the United States and Canada held its 10th Convention in Cairo. Two chartered planes flew to Egypt with the representatives of some seventy-eight thousand Arab Moslems living in the New World. These representatives were welcomed by both the Egyptian government and the American Embassy in Cairo. While the American Embassy welcomed them as American citizens and bearers of good will, the Egyptian government welcomed them as Americans affiliated ethnically and religiously with the Arab world.

Arab Moslems constitute a small but vital minority among the many ethnic groups forming the structure of American culture. Despite the fact that they first immigrated to America in small numbers around the turn of the century, they now number over seventy-eight thousand. From what part of the Arab world have they come? Why did they leave the old country? What attracted them to America? How do they live in the United States? What are the cultural and religious adjustments they had to make in their new environment? How do they fare in a nation composed primarily of European and Christian elements? The adjustment (whether or not it involves "Americanization") of a foreign ethnic group is controlled by racial, religious, and occupational forces. In the Detroit and Toledo Arab Moslem communities, we have two groups from the same cultural origin, yet differing widely in the degree of adjustment and resistance to change. It is hoped that a description of the contrasts between these two communities will dramatize some of the factors of the assimilation of an alien group into American culture.

The Arab Moslems have not followed the typical American "melting pot" pattern of adopting wholeheartedly the ways of the new home. Indeed, they have formed communities in Detroit and Toledo which are rather unique in the history of America. They have kept their individual ethnic-religious patterns without sacrificing the benefits of life in a new world. This book gives a detailed picture of people in an unknown land—the hopes that brought them and the reality they face in building a new life.

The analyses are based on field research conducted in 1959 in the Moslem communities of Toledo, Ohio, and Detroit, Michigan. To keep the material up to date, further investigations and contacts have continued with the leading members of these communities. For the sake of concentration and valid analyses, the non-Arab Moslems (Negroes, Indians, Pakistanis, and Europeans) are not included except for showing the relations between them and the Arab Moslems. The same is the case with the Arab Christians.

Throughout the period of field research and the revision of the original manuscript, the writer has received the constant encouragement and critical advice of many members of the Princeton University faculty. I am especially indebted to Professor Morroe Berger whose patience and generosity in giving of his time, knowledge, and keen critical powers cannot be adequately acknowledged.

My gratitude also goes to Professors Melvin M. Tumin and Wilbert E. Moore, official advisors of the field research, and to Professors Charles F. Westoff and Philip C. Sagi for their help on methodology.

I owe much gratitude to my interviewees as well as to the social and religious leaders in the Toledo and Detroit communities who generously gave their time to be helpful. I must single out in Toledo Sheikh Kamil Y. Avdich, religious leader at the time of the research, and Miss Lila Talip, now Mrs. Joe Aasy, who was an active member of the community. In Detroit, Mrs. Nazmiyyah Aladry, the community's most active member, Mr. Alec Berry, and Mr. Abdallah Berry. Their interest and information are sincerely appreciated.

If I assume that the work involved in this book could have been undertaken without the encouraging interest and aid of my wife I would be very pretentious. For her assistance and encouragement, which has always been given graciously, I extend my gratitude.

Finally, I am indebted to the Dodge Foundation for their generous support for this project.

Contents

List of Tables

CHAPTER ONE

Arab Moslems in America: A Profile

The enormous literature on immigrant groups in the United States has concentrated on either the problem of ethnic maintenance of old traditions in terms of "cultural pluralism" or the question of adjustment to the American culture in the concept of "the melting pot." Aside from the Jewish groups, whose problem is not so much a religious one as it is a consciousness of race, very few intensive studies have probed deeply into the patterns of acculturation and resistance of an immigrant group, alienated culturally and religiously from the newly adopted country.

The many waves of migrations throughout the short history of the United States have not come accidentally from the Western European nations. In fact, they have been attracted to the New World, aside from the economic adventure, by the White Anglo-Saxon Protestants who set the religio-cultural structure of this nation. If the processes of assimilation worked slower among the Eastern and Southern European groups than they did among the Western Europeans in America, it is because of, as maintained by a large number of students of acculturation, the dissimilarities of the economic and social patterns of the countries of origin and the adopted country.

Although the processes of assimilation have not been fully explored, because of the overlapping elements and the various conditions of each element, numerous scholars of assimilation drew a strong negative correlation between religion and assimilation. In other words, adherence to the old religion, which differs from the religion prevailing in the adopted culture, is assumed to delay the immigrant groups in assimilating the values of the new culture. This study will examine this theory as well as illustrate the social conditions under which ethnic-religious groups live in the United States. They are neither Europeans nor Christians, but Arab Moslems.

It is the core of this study that assimilation of an immigrant group is not necessarily hindered by adherence to an original religion differing from the religion prevailing in the adopted culture. Support for this is based on the comparative analysis of two Arab Moslem communities in the United States: one in Toledo, Ohio, and the other in Detroit, Michigan. The data for the analysis were collected chiefly through interviewing the members of a sample picked at random from each community. The data showed the invalidity of assuming an antithesis between assimilation and original religion: the Toledo community was found to be more assimilated than the Detroit community, yet it also proved to be more religious.

Moreover, this study reveals some important variables affecting both the degree of assimilation and religiosity; these may explain the difference between the two communities whose ethnoreligious backgrounds are identical. The different occupational patterns of Toledo and Detroit Moslems were found to be related to the difference in the two communities' assimilation and religiosity. The Toledo community represents the business class, while Detroit represents the working class. The nature of the Toledo business—most of the males in the community are bar owners—has necessitated ecological dispersion of the community. Thus the members, who have become exposed to the American culture in their business and residence, are more assimilated into their new culture than the Detroit members. Working almost solely in the auto factories of Detroit, these Moslems live in a ghetto-like community in Dearborn. Besides delaying the process of assimilation, the residential concentration of the Detroit community has perpetuated the traditional conceptions of family and social relations, as well as of religion and of the sectarian conflict between Sunnis and Shi'ahs. These traditional attitudes of the Detroit community have dissociated the American-born generations from the first-generation immigrants, and an area of cultural discontinuity has thus been created.

The moderate attitudes of the Toledo first-generation immigrants, on the other hand, have helped to bridge the gap between generations, and the community as a whole, through active social participation by the American-born generation, has gained a high degree of assimilation. Exposure to the American culture and awareness of the threat that Christianity poses to their younger generations has enabled the Toledo community, through cooperation between its two sects, to build a common religious front to fortify its faith and preserve its religious identity. Religion in Toledo has been pursued as a means of emulating, and being accepted by, the American socio-economic middle class. Thus, religion has become separate from nationality. The community has even accepted the services of a non-Arab Moslem religious scholar who has skillfully managed to promote the social and religious activities of the community.

The sectarian dispute in Detroit has vitiated religion in the community. In the struggle over social leadership—the same struggle that existed in the old country—the concern of each sect has been not with religion itself, but with Arab nationalism as a means of gaining the traditional support of the authority in the old country.

Most of the Arab Moslems came from Syria and what is politically known now as Lebanon, driven by poverty, attracted by wealth. Their migration to the New World began shortly before the turn of the twentieth century, following the example of their Christian countrymen who had preceded them by some twenty years. Religion was the main factor in delaying their migration and accounts now for their small proportion to the Arab Christians[1] in the U.S.A. "In 1885," says an elderly Moslem woman, "my father planned to accompany some Christian friends to America. He bought the ticket and boarded the boat. Shortly before sailing he asked the captain whether America had mosques. Told that it had none, he feared that America was *bilād kufr* [a land of unbelief]. He immediately got off the boat."

The Quota Law which has been implemented since 1924 is a third factor in limiting their number after they got to know of the United States. A great majority of the Arab emigrants, especially the married and those who could not get sponsors, went to South America.

The first Moslem family settled in Toledo in 1915, after eight years of wandering in the United States. There were two waves of migration to Toledo: from 1945 to 1949, and from 1952 to 1955. The great majority of the Toledo members did not come directly from the old country, as was the case in Detroit, but from within the United States itself. They were mainly attracted to the

[1] Moslems constitute 10 per cent of the Arabs in Toledo and Detroit. This seems also to be roughly the Moslem proportion among Arabs in the U. S. and Latin America, according to various estimates.

city by the liquor business which one Moslem family was said to have entered. This family imported relatives from other states and employed them to meet the business expansion, securing maximum profit with minimum cost in paying wages. But those business-minded relatives very quickly realized the attractive net profits, and thus branched out in the same business direction, helped by the first family. The relatives brought others with them to start the same cycle; the news was spread, and in less than twenty years the Moslems owned 127 of the city's 420 bars, or about 30 per cent, in addition to liquor stores, carry-out businesses, and restaurants with liquor licenses. Some Moslems today have two or three bars. Many retire but keep the bars, either running them through hired workers or subletting them with the reservation of license ownership. Some with high status occupations also indulge in bar ownership, hire help, and invest their outside working hours in the business.

It has become well known in and around Toledo that the city's liquor business is almost monopolized by the Moslems who had actually started this trend by chance, and continued it by profit-orientation, cohesive relationships, and natural jealousy among the relatives to imitate the successful members. The cost of a liquor license has risen in the last ten years from $600 to $20,000 and more on the black market. One of the interviewees said: "Liquor is the most profitable business we have ever experienced. You never lose on it or bear any waste by contamination. To give you just one example, last year I sold in my restaurant whiskey for $11,000. The net profit was $9,000."

As in Toledo, the majority of the Moslems in Detroit came from Lebanon. But there is also a considerable number from Yemen, Iraq, and Syria. There are also some non-Arab Moslems: a small Albanian community with its leader and mosque, some Turkish, Yugoslavian, Indian, Pakistani, and even American Negro Moslems. The different groups do not affiliate themselves with each other, or with the Arab Moslems in Detroit. Except for the friendly personal relations of the Albanian religious leader with some socially prominent Arab Moslems, there is no connection whatsoever between the Arabs and the other ethnic groups.

The city of Detroit is composed of about 40 ethnic groups,[2]

[2] Albert Mayer, *Ethnic Groups in Detroit: 1951*, unpublished mimeograph by Wayne University, Department of Sociology and Anthropology, June 1951.

each of which has one or more of its own churches. Within this ethnic complex, the Moslem Arabs stress that they are Arabs. In fact, the relationship between the Arab Moslem community and the Arab Christian community, which is ten times larger than the Moslem community, is very much stronger than that between the Arab Moslem community and the other non-Arab Moslem communities in Detroit.

Most of the members of the Detroit Moslem community are engaged in factory work at auto plants; this is the main occupation for the other ethnic groups as well. As in Toledo, the Christian Arabs were pioneers in starting the community in the 1880's, to be followed about 15 years later by the Moslems. The peak of migration to Detroit had two periods: between 1927 and 1933, and between 1946 and 1953. The majority of the immigrants came directly from the old country and remained in the city.

Detroit has two mosques and one national religious club or, as some count them, three mosques. Of these three mosques, one belongs to the Albanian Moslems. The other two are for the Arab Moslems; one is for the Shi'ah sect and is called "The Arabian-Hashimite Club" (al-Nādī al-'arabī al-Hashimī). It is a few yards away from the third mosque, that of the Sunni sect. The existence of the two Arab mosques is a sign of the persisting sectarianism, carried over from the old country by the first-generation immigrants and still maintained, between Shi'ah and Sunni. Although it exists in Toledo, this sectarian difference is not noticed there at all; the reasons for this will be explained later. In 1964, an Islamic Center was built in Detroit.

CHAPTER TWO

Historical Background and Present Situations

The members of the two Moslem communities included in this study are all Arabs either by birth or origin, most of them from Lebanon, but a few families from Syria and Palestine, and all now American citizens either by naturalization or birth. To shed some light on the subsequent analyses, we must understand some of the prevailing social as well as religious conditions in their country of origin during the last half of the nineteenth century, when the Moslems started to learn about America.

Four Moslem Sects in the Old Country

In 1860, John Wortabet[1] drew his rough sketch of Syria's population by religious sects:

Greek Orthodox	150,000	
Greek Catholic	50,000	
Maronites	200,000	
Jews	30,000	
Nusairiyeh	200,000	1,080,000
Druzes	50,000	
Metawileh	80,000	
Mohammedans	750,000	
Total	1,510,000	

The last four sects are Moslem and total 1,080,000 persons or more than two-thirds of the whole Syrian population at that time. The religion of Nusairiyeh, although Islam, seems to bear a close affinity, in its general principles, to that of the Druzes. There is no need to mention the doctrines of these two sects since no single member was met in either community. However, the Shi'ahs and Sunnis, which Wortabet called "Metawileh and Mo-

[1] John Wortabet, *Research into the Religions of Syria: Sketches, Historical and Doctrinal, of Its Religious Sects* (London: Nisbet and Co., 1860), p. ix.

hammedans," generally do not mix or intermarry with the other two sects. Wortabet's table shows that the Shi'ahs are approximately one-tenth of the Sunnis. As our concern is with the religious differences between these two sects, it is proper here to give a brief history of the Shi'ah development.

The Shi'ah sect started in Islam as early as 10 A.H. (632 A.D.), or immediately after the death of the Prophet Muhammad. Its appearance marked the first schism in Islam, and was caused by the political question of who had the right to succeed the Prophet. One party rallied around Abu Bakr, the first person who responded to Islam, and the Prophet's companion in the Hegira from Mecca to Medina; another party followed Ali, the Prophet's cousin and the husband of his favorite daughter, Fatima. At first, the party of Abu Bakr prevailed and succeeded in electing not only him but the two succeeding caliphs, Omar and Othman. Indeed, Ali became the fourth caliph, twenty-three years after the death of the Prophet. But the revolt of the Mu'awiyah party provoked a long and bloody conflict which marked the first true schism in Islam. Ali was killed. He was succeeded by his older son, Hasan, who soon abdicated in favor of Mu'awiyah to preserve the unity of Islam. However, the conflict continued, and Hussein, the brother of Hasan, was killed on the field of Karbala. Ever since, this field has been sacred ground to the Shi'ahs or partisans of the family of Ali. The political split then became final.

With the Shi'ahs, the term *Imamate* takes the place of the Sunni term *Caliphate*. But the main body of Shi'ahs believe in an hereditary line of twelve Imams. The first was Ali; the last was the child of Hasan-el-'Askari, Muhammad, who disappeared from sight in 878 A.D., but who is still supposed to be living in the world in a disguise which is revealed only rarely. But among the Shi'ahs themselves, the very question of the Imamate produced a schism from which the Isma'iliyah, the Druzes, and the Assassins emerged.

In the old country, the two sects rarely intermarry. The Shi'ahs repudiate the first three caliphs: Abu Bakr, Omar, and Othman. They especially hate Omar and cannot even stand the name. The American-born Shi'ahs have moderate attitudes toward the Sunnis. This is perhaps a result of two factors: the weakness in their religious instructions and practices; and realization of the threat of Christianity. However, most of the first-generation Shi'ahs still hate Omar. A contemporary Moslem scholar once went to Detroit and sold many copies of his book about the history of Islam. A Shi'ah member bought two copies. Not knowing how to read, he asked his daughter to read the contents of the book to him. She mentioned a chapter about "Omar and his merits"; he asked her to stop, and he immediately took the two copies back to the writer, saying, "Keep the money, God bless you, but please take back your books. Omar and I cannot stay together in one home."

As in the old country, most of the first-generation Shi'ahs do not eat of animals killed by aliens. In the Toledo and Detroit communities, they go to the slaughterhouse themselves, slaughter their animals, and distribute them among their members.

The differences between the Sunni and Shi'ah religious practices are mainly confined to minor details of rituals. In the call to prayer, the Shi'ahs insert twice before the end "Hayy 'Ala khir 'Amal," which means "hurry to perform the best deed." There is some variation in the ceremony of ablution before prayer. For example, the Sunni lets the water run from his hand down the arm to the elbow; the Shi'ah reverses the process, so that the water runs from the elbow to the hand. For the sake of convenience, the Shi'ahs may combine the noon prayer with the afternoon worship, and the sunset prayer with the evening prayer. In response to the conventional question, "How many times a day should a good Moslem pray?" the Sunnis answered five times, while the great majority of the Shi'ahs said three times. Also, the Shi'ahs give no special prominence to the Friday noon service, which they said need not even have a sermon. They always favor praying singly, unlike the Sunnis who favor praying in a group. The Shi'ahs, therefore, do not favor building mosques in America, but rather, national clubs. They did this in Detroit and tried unsuccessfully to do so in Toledo.

The Arab Moslems Learning about America

The Arab Moslems learned about America around the turn of the twentieth century, after it had been discovered twenty-five years earlier by the Arab Christians. The reason that the Moslems were later than the Christians in immigrating to America lay in the religious difference. The fear of losing their religion in the unbelieving country was the main factor delaying the Moslems a quarter of a century in their immigration in groups to America.

A migration, however, is nothing new to Moslems. From the early days of Islam they experienced several types of migration. Before the migration of all the Moslems from Mecca to Medina in 621 A.D., the Moslems migrated twice in large groups to Abyssinia between 615 and 619 A.D. They felt closer to the Christian king of Abyssinia at that time than to their pagan kin in Arabia who persecuted them because of their new faith. Other migrations were occasioned by military conquest of Asia, Africa, and Europe as well as by commercial interests. Moreover, as nomads, the Arabs even long before Islam knew no political boundaries to limit their economic activities and their search for water and pasture. That social background of their nomadic life made the Arabs successful merchants and taught them to adjust quickly to other cultures. To this characteristic Islam owed the Arabs a great deal of its expansion all over the world. Islam also absorbed various cultures, which adopted the religion in the first half-century of its expansion. In terms of the number of its followers, Islam today is one of the largest religions. It has over 400,000,000 members who are geographically distributed[2] as follows: North America, 33,000;[3] South America, 342,615; Europe, 12,425,300; Asia, 321,524, 930; Africa, 86,178,853; Oceania, 102,000.

The Moslems in America

North America (the United States and Canada) is the Moslems' most recent area of settlement. The distribution of the Moslems in America is unknown, since there is no census taken

[2] *The World Almanac and Book of Facts for 1960*, New York: New York World-Telegram, 1960, p. 715.

[3] Other estimates, however, range as high as 250,000 (see "Races" in *Time*, August 10, 159, pp. 24-25.). Mr. T. Graves of the U.S.I.A. in his unpublished "The Muslim in America Stories," estimated the number at 60,000. Nadim Makdisi in his "The Moslems of America," in the *Christian Century*, August 26, 1959, pp. 969-71, and in his "The Muslims of America," in *The Islamic Review* (Woking, England [June 1955]), pp. 28-32, estimated the number at 80,000. C. Umhau Wolf in his "Muslims In The American Mid-West," in *The Muslim World*, January 1960, pp. 39-48, estimated the number "from 50,000 to 80,000 with the realistic figure near the high side."

This writer separates the Moslems in America into three categories: Arab Moslems with an estimated number of 78,000; non-Arab Moslems (excluding American Negroes) with the estimated number of 30,000; and American Negro "Muslims" with an estimated number of 70,000. See the foregoing.

by religion except the "Religious Bodies: 1936"[4] which gives no information whatsoever about the Moslems in America. The lack of information about this religious group is due to its small number and recent migration, as well as to the apparent absence of a central body.[5] Though the Islamic Center in Washington, D.C., and the Islamic Federation were both created in 1952, they have not yet functioned as agencies of information concerning the activities of Moslems. In fact, both of these organizations know very little about the exact number and distribution of the Moslems in America. Arab Moslems are scattered throughout all the states but concentrated in the industrial metropolitan areas of New York, Chicago, and Detroit. The rough estimate of the number and distribution of the Arab Moslems in America is given by some expert members, Arabic newspaper owners, and religious leaders in the Toledo and Detroit communities as follows:

Michigan	14,000
New York	14,000
Illinois	11,000
Ohio	3,600
Indiana	3,200
Iowa	2,000
California	2,000
Virginia	1,800
Connecticut	1,700
South Dakota	1,500
Oklahoma	1,400
Massachusetts	1,400
Georgia	1,200
Kentucky	1,200
Kansas	1,000
Minnesota	1,000
Other States	6,000
Canada	10,000
	78,000

There are, in addition, some 30,000 Moslems of nationality other than Arab, such as Indians, Albanians, Yugoslavians, and Turks. Sacramento has a large Moslem community with the first

[4] U. S. Bureau of the Census, *Religious Bodies: 1936* (Washington, D.C.: Government Printing Office, 1941), Vols. I-II.

[5] *Yearbook of American Churches for 1960*, ed. Benson Y. Landis (New York, 1959), p. 85.

mosque on the West Coast. In general, California has the largest number of the Indian Moslems, most of whom are farmers who came in 1906 from the Punjab and Northwest Frontier region of what is now Pakistan. With regard to missionary activities, the Indian Moslems are the most active in the United States. They have a magazine called *Muslim Sunrise* printed in Washington, D.C. Most of them belong to the American Fazl Mosque which has missions in all parts of the world and in Pittsburgh, Chicago, New York, and Los Angeles. This mosque is connected with the Ahmadiyya Movement in Islam founded in India in 1879 by Mirza Ghulam Ahmad (who died in 1908) for a "reinterpretation of Islam," to uplift humanity and spread peace through the world.

In addition to these 100,000 Moslems in the United States, there are about 70,000 Negroes who call themselves "Muslims." These are the followers of Elijah Muhammad who claims 250,000 Negro communicants from Harlem to Los Angeles. This Negro religious movement seems to have stemmed from the Ahmadiyya missionary work, but was modified by Elijah to attract Negroes resentful of the discrimination they suffer. Obviously, this growing Negro religious movement has been influenced by the Moslem migration from India. What attracted them to Islam was its principle of social equality as a rapid means of economic and social emancipation. But, paradoxically enough, they twisted its principle of equality to "black supremacy." This is why the Arab Moslems in America dissociate themselves from the Black Muslims and consider them a great danger to themselves as well as to Islam. The Black Muslims seem to have been exploited by their religious leaders who manipulate the Negro's hatred of the white man as a reaction to discrimination. However, it is hoped that through true Islamic education this movement would be corrected along the right Islamic path of complete equality and human brotherhood.[6]

The Mosque Institution

America has twelve mosques and one Islamic center, with another in prospect. The first mosque in America was built in Highland Park, Michigan, in 1919. It is now a church. The second mosque, which still exists, was built in Michigan City, Indiana,

[6] One of Elijah Muhammad's sons, Akbar Muhammad, is now in Cairo attending Al-Azhar University. He is expected to take over the religious leadership of the Black Muslim movement after his father.

in 1924. There are mosques in Cedar Rapids, Iowa; Chicago, Illinois; Dearborn and Detroit, Michigan; Toledo, Ohio; Sacramento, California; and London, Ontario, in Canada.

Although the mosque in Islam does not have exclusively religious significance, since the Moslem can pray on any clean spot on the earth, it became very significant in the Moslem community life in America. Here the mosque is the center of religious and social life as well as a liaison between the larger society and the Moslem community. The mosque in the community is the center of many social activities. It is even "the place of social gossip," as a young woman critically put it. The women gather every now and then in the office of the *sheikh* (religious leader) to exchange gossip about the members of their community and other communities in America and overseas. In other communities, if someone marries, dies, if the community intends to give a party for any prominent Arab personality, in general, if any news need be publicized, the mosque is the center for disseminating such news. Besides the religious activities and Friday group prayer (equivalent to Sunday church ceremonies for the Christians), the mosque is the place for funeral ceremonies, wedding parties, religious festivals, and all social as well as political events. Every month the community holds a dinner at the mosque; very often on such occasions one community invites other communities.

As the liaison between the community and the larger society, the mosque enables the other religious and ethnic groups to get to know a great deal about the Arab Moslem community; a measurable degree of mutual religious understanding and social cooperation is thus obtained between the Arab Moslem community and the larger society. About once a week, the religious leader of the community is invited by different churches and social groups to speak about Islam. Many church and social groups go to the mosque where they hear about Islam and see films about the culture of the Middle East.

As an educational institution, the mosque plays an important role among the new Moslem generation, transmitting the cultural and religious values and teaching of Islam. "Sunday school" is held at the mosque. It graduates vigorous Moslems proud of their culture, tradition, and religion. They learn how to be good American citizens living up to the humane religious creed of Islam.

The mosque also serves as a guest house, an institution well known in Arab settlements but not located in the mosque. In the summer of 1958, for example, some Indian Moslem students were touring the Midwest. They knew of the Moslem community and, while they were visiting Toledo, went to the mosque where they were given hospitality. As foreign students with very limited means, they were offered free accommodations at the mosque and invited to dinner by some members of the community. Here the mosque was a cultural medium between the foreign Moslems and the American Moslems.

Toledo and Detroit: A Comparison

Toledo is a middle-sized city in northwest Ohio, near the Michigan border. Toledo's population was estimated to be 339,142 in 1958.[7] Of its population, 91.3 per cent are American-born. Among the foreign-born, Germans and Poles are most numerous. The Syrian Christian community is around 8,400, or slightly more than two per cent of the total population while the Arab Moslem community contains about 260 families, or 1,200 persons. The Toledo Moslem community is thus about four-tenths of one per cent of the total population of the city, but more prominent than its size indicates.

In the past fifty years, Detroit has grown rapidly from 285,704 in 1900 to a population of 1,849,568, or 3,016,197 for its metropolitan area in 1950, to become the fifth largest city in the United States.[8] This growth is associated with the motor vehicle industry. More than 40 per cent of its population are either foreign-born or natives of foreign-born parents.[9] With its 40 ethnic groups, Detroit may be said to have the largest number of foreign groups gathered in one single city in the United States.

One of these 40 groups is the "Syrian," made up of 50,000 people. Though called Syrian, the great majority are of Lebanese descent. About 6,000, or 10 per cent, are Moslems, the majority of whom live together in Dearborn in an area marked by the boundary of Eagle Street to West Fort between Dix and West Vernon Highway. The Detroit Syrian community was started by the Arab Christians in the 1880's, followed by the Moslems around

[7] *Data Book*, Toledo-Lucas County Plan Commission, Toledo, Ohio, July 1958, p. 1.

[8] *Statistical Abstract of the United States*, 1959, U. S. Department of Commerce, Bureau of the Census, Washington, D.C., p. 21.

[9] *World Almanac* for 1959, p. 268.

TABLE 1

Generational Composition of Toledo and Detroit

Generation	*Toledo*		*Detroit*	
	No.	%	No.	%
First	86	41	60	28
Second	97	46	102	49
Third	28	13	49	23
Total	211	100	211	100

the beginning of the twentieth century. The Detroit Moslem community was established much earlier than the Toledo community. It is perhaps the oldest Arab Moslem community in the United States. There is a young fourth generation, but the investigator had no chance to include them in the sample since they are still under fifteen years of age. The first generation in Detroit is now much smaller than in Toledo and it is about to vanish. Table 1 shows the generational distribution of the respondents in both communities. The age distribution (Table 2) shows an expected rapid growth especially in the Detroit community.

THE MOSLEM FAMILY IN AMERICA

The family pattern of these two communities is approximately American. The wife is not merely the equal of her husband; she also dominates family life. This is due not only to the economic participation of the wife in the new world, for two-thirds are housewives, but to the break-up of the patriarchal, extended family. This development of Moslem family life in America has meant a rise in the wife's status in the smaller nuclear family. Moreover, her economic functions in the home in the new environment have made her an equal partner in the entire family enterprise, and Moslem husbands have quickly realized this

TABLE 2

Age Distribution of the Sample in Toledo and Detroit

Age	15–19	20–24	25–29	30–34	35–39	40–44	45–49	50–59	60–69	70+	Total
Toledo	23	20	31	39	31	19	14	11	16	7	211
Detroit	36	23	39	18	14	21	31	15	7	7	211
Total	59	43	70	57	45	40	35	26	23	14	422

change in their wives' position and outlook. Moslem wives also help their husbands in business.

The child in the American Moslem family is looked upon with great solicitude as the person who will enjoy the happy, comfortable life the parents were deprived of in the old country. Thus the child is prepared to lead an independent life guided by the American style of individualism; he is not looked upon as a means of security in the parents' old age, as in the old country. This change in the child's status in the Moslem family in America is influenced by the American socio-economic structure whereby the security for the aged rests more on the state than on kinship. Life insurance and increased capacity for saving among Moslem families also have some connection with the new outlook on children.

"We want our children to enjoy a better life than we led," explained a first-generation respondent. "America is the paradise for women and children!" said another. Children are not expected to contribute to the family's support as in the old traditional culture. This individualistic style has weakened the traditionally intimate family relationship in the second and third Moslem generations in the new world. In Detroit, however, some young married couples still share their parents' household, but the patriarchal authority of the head of the house is weak even over the unmarried children.

Marriage

Among the first and second generation in Toledo and Detroit, the husband and wife call each other "my cousin" even if they are not actually related to each other. This refers to the traditional and prevailing custom of first cousin marriage in the Middle East. There a man may not be denied if he chooses to marry his first cousin. Unless he declares his precise intention to the contrary, his cousin is held for him and no other man may marry her. The Christians in the Middle East do not differ from the Moslems in this respect. This traditional custom is carried over to the new world by the first generation, among whom a high percentage of first cousin marriages are found. A Christian Arab member of the faculty of a prominent American university, for example, has told the writer of an incident which took place in America, illustrating the strength of the custom. When his sister was engaged to be married, his cousin, also a United States resident, became angry and asserted in a letter his traditional right to marry the girl. But the Western-minded professor rejected this claim and a serious family dispute followed. The girl herself, partly to restore peace and partly because she herself recognized the tradition to some extent, suggested that her cousin assume a guardianship role in which he, rather than her brother, gives his explicit consent to the marriage.

Mixed Marriage

The mixed marriage is one of the most important agencies of assimilation. It is strongly resisted in both communities when a Moslem girl marries a non-Moslem. If the husband adopts Islam, he is accepted as a full member by the Toledo community but not by the Detroit community. It is not socially desirable for a Moslem young man to marry a non-Moslem girl, for the rest of the community will feel somewhat restricted in dealing with its member who has married an American. As one respondent put it, concerning one such case, "The poor boy cannot invite anyone to dinner before he gives his wife a call. We cannot pass by or drop in as we do with each other. We have to call up beforehand and when we visit him we don't feel at ease because his wife cannot participate in either our conversation or gossip." Thus the strange spouse is felt to hinder the course of ordinary social relations. But however undesirable both communities consider it, they do not openly oppose the marriage.

Such marriages have two stages and sometimes three: the civil ceremony, then the religious one by the sheikh, and sometimes the American family of the bride or the bride herself insists on a third wedding ceremony in the church. Often, however, the couple is satisfied with the civil wedding and omits both religious ceremonies.

The wedding festivities depend upon the class and wealth of both families. I had a chance to attend a wedding party in the Detroit community. The groom was a second generation Moslem, the girl was an American. The party took place at the Knights of Columbus Club. There were over five hundred people invited, most of them Arabs. Many of the Toledo community families attended. After the dinner, there was music and dancing of two kinds: Western music and dancing for the bride's people, and Arabic music with the traditional *Dabka* dance for the Arabs. These two kinds alternated with each other. In the basement, meanwhile, two kinds of drinks were served: soft drinks for the older Arab generation and cocktails for the Americans and the younger Arabs, who outdid the Americans. Many of the younger Arab generation members got drunk but retained sufficient control of themselves not to cause a disturbance. Most of the older generation members left early so as not to cramp the style of the younger generation. Shortly after midnight the party was over and the couple left for their new home to start a new life.

Courtship and Mixed Religious and Racial Marriage

Despite the relatively short period they have been in this country, the Moslems have adopted a liberal attitude toward interreligious marriage. They still, however, feel strongly opposed to their women marrying non-Moslems, as shown in Table 3. This liberal attitude toward interreligious marriage may be the result of the decline in the number of the first generation. The second and third generations tend to intermarry with the Americans. The liberal attitude, moreover, seems also to be a reaction against the former intransigence which led to losses in the community through absolute rejection of young women who married non-Moslems. Through the moderate approach the community retains a hold on its members. Table 4 shows the degree of heterogeneity achieved by both communities in less than six decades.

In contrast to the mixed religious marriage, both communities are very rigid concerning mixed marriage with Negroes. During the long period of the field research, the writer never heard of nor encountered any case of an Arab being married to a Negro.

Conflict between generations in the two communities manifests itself in the changing customs of courtship. The traditionalist community of Detroit still adheres to the values of consanguinity, which dictates that marriage is not a personal matter but a kinship affair in which the members of the two families are involved in reciprocal social obligations. Hence the decision as to whom

TABLE 3

Moslem Attitude toward Females Marrying Non-Moslems, in Per Cent

*Community**	*Oppose*	*Approve on condition*	*Approve without condition*	*Total*
Toledo	48	33	19	100
Detroit	45	25	30	100

* N = 211 in each community.

TABLE 4
Percentage Distribution of Marriage, According to Religion of the Spouse, by Area

Area	*Both Moslems*	*One Christian*	*One Jewish*	*Total*
Toledo	71	25	4	100
Detroit	71	28	1	100

one will marry is not up to the individual. It is treated on a family level and is often fixed by the two families. Maintaining the traditional sectarian conflict, the Detroit families of each sect, Shi'ah and Sunni, do not encourage their children to intermarry. The older generation members try to marry their children to partners from friendly families of the same sect. The children resent this and many are therefore driven to marry outside the community.

In Toledo, where sectarianism is weak, cross-sect marriage is more common. Marriage itself is regarded as a personal matter—one of mutual understanding between two persons—and is not limited by either religion or nationality. Both courtship and marriage take the American form, based on romantic love. But despite the overtly Americanized attitudes concerning courtship and marriage, the ratio of the homogeneous marriage in Toledo is higher than in Detroit, 5 to 4, as shown in Table 5. The percentage of the Toledo second generation who are married to Moslems is higher than in Detroit, as shown in Table 6. And more third-generation members in Toledo than in Detroit are engaged to Moslems, as shown in Table 7.

The explanation of this preference in the frequency of mixed marriages lies in the religious activities in both communities. The religious institutions in the Toledo community enable the young

TABLE 5
Distribution of Respondents on Religious Marriage, by Community

Religion of Spouse	*Toledo*		*Detroit*	
	No.	%	No.	%
Both Moslem	125	59.2	105	49.8
One Christian	41	19.4	45	21.3
One Jewish	3	1.4	2	0.9
Not married	42	20.0	59	28.0
Total	211	100.0	211	100.0

TABLE 6

Distribution of Respondents on Religious Marriage in the Two Communities, by Generation

Religion of Spouse	*Third*		*Second*		*First*	
	T	D	T	D	T	D
Both Moslem	0	0	59	54	80	80
One Christian	27	30	27	21	9	14
One Jewish	0	3	3	1	3	0
Not married	73	67	11	24	8	6
Total	100	100	100	100	100	100

people of both sexes to meet in an harmonious, favorable, and intimate way. Their Americanized religious activities, such as publishing religious material, holding conferences, and sponsoring parties, raise their prestige and self-esteem. These promoted religious activities acquaint the Moslem youth with one another and with the Moslem youth in other communities, although friendly relations with other religious groups are not excluded.

The Toledo youth are encouraged by their parents and religious leader to make the mosque the headquarters for their social activities. The mosque has thus become not only the place for worship and religious instructions but also the popular place for the youth where American social activities range from dating to mixed dancing. The older-generation parents do not object to their daughters dancing at such affairs with Moslem boys.

Such parties are held in the mosque's basement. The same loudspeaker which broadcasts the recorded Quranic verses before Friday prayer now broadcasts rock-and-roll music for the third generation and waltzes for the second. In contrast, the only dance that the Detroit first generation allow their youth to perform in

TABLE 7

Distribution of the Third Generation Members in the Two Communities Engaged to be Married

Religion of Fiancé	*Toledo*		*Detroit*	
	No.	%	No.	%
Moslem	9	37.5	7	24.1
Non-Moslem	4	16.6	8	27.7
Not engaged	11	45.9	14	48.2
Total	24	100.0	29	100.0

their mosque's basement is the traditional *Dabka*, in which the group of men and women hold their hands in a large circle and collectively move from right to left in a six-step unit. This kind of folk dance, carried over from the old country, reflects the co-operative community pattern of the relatively self-sufficient agrarian societies. The accompanying loud music, whose theme is brief but often repeated, pains the American-born third generation who are used to a different kind of music.

The different kinds of permissible social activities in the mosques of the two communities illustrate two concepts of the mosque institution in the minds of the youth. To the Detroit youth, the mosque is an "old-fashioned" institution which reflects the unpleasant conceptions about the old country as "a place of poor, uneducated people with 'old-fashioned' ideas about relations between men and women or between parents and children."[10] The mosque has become for the youth an institution with no appealing functions. Whenever they go to the mosque, once or twice a year for the two feast prayers, they can hardly understand the traditional rituals the old-fashioned *imam* performs. Neither do they understand his preaching in bad Arabic, read from a book dating back several hundred years.

To the Toledo youth, the mosque is an expansion of their community and social life. The imam was not imposed upon the community to perform the traditional ritual functions but, rather, was selected for his ability to serve the social purposes set forth by the leading second-generation members. The youth express pride, therefore, in both their imam and their mosque. They do not hesitate to invite their American schoolmates and friends to the mosque to talk to their imam. The American flag alongside the Islamic flag on the sides of the niche symbolizes the conceptual amalgamation of Islam with Americanization. To these youth, Islam is universal but its traditions are peculiar features of specific cultures. Their concern is with Islam as a whole—with how to apply its general rules in the new environment rather than to shape the new environment to the particular traditionalistic instructions and customs.

This problem of applying Islam's general tenets to many different cultures is not strange to Islam as a social system. In fact, Islam owes its cultural richness to the many different cultural

[10] Morroe Berger, "Americans From the Arab World," in James Kritzeck and R. Bayly Winder (eds.), *The World of Islam* (New York, 1959), p. 368.

elements it has absorbed. Since the dawn of Islam, even during the period of revelation, religious instructions have been adjusted to the changing social and economic conditions. After the *Hegira* (flight) to Medina, the Prophet, waiving a previous ruling, permitted *al-salam* in which one could sell his expected crops in advance. He also adopted some Jewish religious practices, such as fasting on *Yawm ʻashuraa.* When the new Moslem generations in America share with the prevailing Christian population the celebration of Christmas, they feel it is analogous with the Prophet's sharing with the Jews of Medina the fasting of *Yawm ʻashuraa.*

The flexible tenets of Islam are the very substance of its capacity to function within any social structure. Rigidity in religion was very much disliked by the Prophet. On his way to perform a part of the pilgrimage, for example, he advised his companions to shift the hours of prayer.

The gulf between generations in the Toledo and Detroit communities reflects a general condition in America, not merely that in any immigrant community. As two social scientists have put it, "Each generation of Americans has come to a new world and has lived to see much of it outmoded."[11]

Divorce

Divorce in both communities follows American procedures, which differ from one state to another. With Moslem couples, especially among the first generation, the wife never uses her American right to divorce her husband, since in traditional Islam, unless otherwise specified in the marriage contract, only the husband has the right to divorce. The first-generation woman still looks upon divorce as equivalent to social and economic death. This conception is the product of the economic structure of the Middle East, which still depends heavily on male skill and training in all occupations. The scarcity of economic opportunities restricts women to the home, and a career girl or career woman is an outlandish conception for the Eastern woman. Thus an Eastern woman, dependent on her husband in every way, is willing to bear the family hardship and sometimes the improper conduct of her husband without taking a judicial action for divorcing him.

[11] Daniel R. Miller and Guy E. Swanson, *The Changing American Parent: A Study in the Detroit Area* (New York, 1958), p. 236.

When the husband initiates divorce proceedings in an American court, he leaves the home to the wife and seeks other accommodations for himself. Throughout the period of the divorce procedures, the members of the community try to persuade the husband to drop the case and go back to his wife. Even after the court grants a divorce, the community's first-generation members continue to persuade the husband to keep the marital bonds, as if the court decision had not affected the marriage. They argue that the marriage was religiously established by the sheikh, and since it is not religiously terminated by the sheikh, it still exists and the court decision is void and they are, as Moslems, not bound by it. The husband, who bore the court expense, of course, does not listen to such arguments. He gives his ex-wife the household plus what the court gave her as compensation. The compensation often attracts someone else from the surrounding communities to marry the divorced woman; if not, she goes back to the old country to remarry.

Moslem divorce in the United States has a two-fold social significance: (1) the husband follows American legal proceedings and does not use his religious right of oral divorce; (2) the first-generation members of the community consider the divorce granted by the American court void, and they try to persuade the husband to retain his divorced wife. However, divorce is rare in the two communities.

Social Relations with the Arab Christians

The social relations between Moslems and the Arab Christians differ in the two communities. In Toledo, the economic status of the Moslems is, in general, higher than that of the Arab Christians and the latter envy the former because of their economic success. The investigator experienced an extreme example of this feeling. After interviewing a Moslem wife in her bar, the investigator was followed outside by an Arab Christian customer. The customer started chatting with the investigator, directing his attention to the Moslems' deviation from their traditional religion. "Did you see what these people do here?" he asked, "They own most of the bars in Toledo. Not only that, they have their wives work with them as bartenders. These dirty people are now the wealthiest in the city, but they are not satisfied. They achieved their wealth by selling liquor. As you saw that lady had uncovered hair and arms. Her husband, according to Islam, is not supposed to expose her that way to strangers, but they forgot everything about tradition and religion because of the dollar." Despite this kind of economic jealousy, there is a kind of courtesy between the two groups. In Toledo, the Arab Moslems often take part in the social events of the Arab Christians in their churches. There are frequent visits between the families of both groups. At weddings or funerals the two groups get together. Whenever any prominent Arab personality is invited by the Moslem community, the Arab Christian community takes part in the reception. For any social or religious event in each community, the other community feels obligated to participate.

But in Detroit, relations between the two groups are very limited. There is a kind of friction between the two groups and sometimes they take opposite nationalistic points of view. When the Prime Minister of Lebanon came to the United States in the fall of 1959, the Detroit community wanted to invite him for a visit. As the Arab Christians in Detroit are, in general, more socially prominent, than the Moslems, the Moslem community suggested to an Arab Christian judge that he direct the community invitation to Rashīd Karamī. It was later discovered that his invitation was a personal one, used to gain prestige for himself through his position in the community. A socially active woman in the Moslem community wrote to me: "We blamed him for this but he was stubborn. Then the Moslem society gathered immediately and sent the Prime Minister a community invitation to which he responded. We gave him a nice reception and as usual none of the Arab Christians showed up." These mutually uncooperative attitudes in Detroit have blocked the many attempts to fully utilize America's Arab population on ethnic and nationalistic grounds to offset the Zionist propaganda in America. The Arab Convention of 1957 in Detroit did not encourage sponsors to arrange for another. It is one of the new goals of the Islamic Federation to construct an Arab solidarity in the United States, but it is very unlikely that the Arab Christians will be willing to cooperate with the Arab Moslems, for the Arab Christians feel more affiliated with the American society and the Western world than with the Moslems or the Arab world. In addition, the Christian community in Detroit is so torn apart because of the sectarian dispute between the many denominations that there is no major cooperation.

Relations between the Moslems and Other Religious Groups

The social relations between the Moslems in the two communities and other American religious groups is almost unilateral, in the sense that the other religious groups are much more interested in learning about the Moslems than the Moslems are in learning about them. Perhaps this is because Islam came historically after the two main religions, Judaism and Christianity, and thus the Moslems feel they know enough about both religions, while Islam in America is still not known to a great many religious groups.

Outside religious groups come to the mosque in both communities about once a week. In the Toledo community they are received by the religious leader who speaks to them or has one of his students give the speech in his presence. Due to its lack of an educated religious leader at the time of the research, the Detroit community very often must use one of the many Arab students studying at the University of Michigan. This university has a new religious organization called "Moslem Student Association," capable of fulfilling the occasional community need for a speaker on Islam.

In Toledo, the religious leader is occasionally invited outside by the other social and religious groups to speak about Islam. He also feeds the local press with news of his community and of religious events, indicating their social significance. An example is the following published announcement on the front page of the Toledo *Blade*.[12]

TOLEDO MOSLEMS OBSERVE RAMADAN

30-Day Fasting Period Started

Members of the Toledo Moslem Community have begun their annual 30-day period of fasting in observance of Ramadan, a solemn season which commemorates the beginning of the Moslem faith through the prophet Muhammad.

Rules of the fast provide for abstinence from food, drink and other physical pleasures from sunrise (it is from dawn) to sunset daily. The fast will conclude April 8.

Ramadan also is the name of the ninth month in the Islamic calendar.

Imam Kamil Avdich, leader of the Toledo community which has about 300 families, explained that the rigid requirements of

[12] March 12, 1959.

the fast provide "a way to elevate ourselves spiritually and to prove that the human body is not the master, but servant of the human spirit."

Such frequent publicity familiarizes the larger society with the Moslem community, and explaining Moslem rituals in this way gives the community a kind of social prestige.

This social prestige of religion in the Toledo community is sought through Arab nationalism in Detroit. The Detroit community, for example, was aroused by an article published in the Detroit *Free Press* on September 22, 1953, by the columnist Robert C. Ruark, under the heading, "The Arab Poses a Problem." The columnist attacked the Arabs as "probably the most expert and persistent thieves in the world," because "basically" they are all Moslems and "live by Koranic law, or indirect personal applications of it, with no respect for modern adaptation of civil law." The Detroit Moslem community collected around $1,000 with which it bought space in the Detroit *News* of October 16, 1953, and published a sharp reply to Mr. Ruark's article. The reply made clear that

> Islam and the Arabs were responsible for one of the greatest civilizations that existed. A large measure of Western civilization owes its heritage to the Moslem and Arab world in the past. Arabic was the medium for expounding on Greek philosophy, science, which the Arab preserved, enlarged upon and handed down to the Western world. These people dealt in medicine, chemistry, mathematics and geography. . . . Your gross misrepresentation of an area and its people and religions do not help our country (America) gain much-needed friends, especially in such a key area as the Middle East.
>
> Respectfully,
> Arab-American Friendship Federation
> 9940 Burley Street
> Dearborn, Michigan

The significance of the article and the reply lies in the following. First, the community in Detroit does not have as much social prestige as that in Toledo; if it did, the press would not have published such an article or, even after the publication, would have expressed its apology by publishing the Arabs' reply free of charge.

Second, the lack of religious leadership in the Detroit community meant a communications vacuum between itself and the press in which the latter did not find a community representative to consult. In Toledo, the press consults the religious leader in such matters and, because of the excellent communication and good relations between the community representative and the press, such an attack would probably not appear in the Toledo press.

Third, had such an attack appeared in the Toledo press anyway, the reply would have appeared the following day and not, as in Detroit, after 24 days. The lapse of time between the appearance of Ruark's article and the reply shows the loose organization in the community. The clear division of functions in the Toledo community provides for quick action. In Detroit, every event requires the ad hoc formation of an organization to deal with the situation and this takes so much time that the occasion is often forgotten before the action is taken.

Family Interrelations in Both Communities

In Toledo the office of religious leadership affects communication between the community and the larger society. Also influential are the family interrelations in both communities. The Toledo community is interrelated through five large main families. All but three of the nucleus families are related by marriage, agnation, or cognation. These cohesive kin relations give the community a unified view in dealing with any problem regarding the outside world. The members of the community tend to see these problems in the same way.

Family interrelations in the Detroit community are less cohesive. This weakness has led to an individualistic approach to outside problems rather than seeing them as the concern of the community as a whole. Each subgroup in Detroit judges issues from the narrow angle of how much the subgroup is going to benefit over the others. This situation was emphasized during the visit of King Hussein of Jordan to Detroit on April 12, 1959. Because of his political dispute at that time with President Nasser of the United Arab Republic, the Detroit community decided to demonstrate against King Hussein at the Detroit Airport. But the governor of Michigan wanted to welcome him as an official guest of the United States. Furthermore, he wanted to do so to make a good impression on the Arab community. But the community refused the indirect overtures of the governor and declared its intention to demonstrate peacefully against the king's policy. The governor got in touch with some leaders in the community and they in turn contacted their groups, and the governor thus managed to win over a part of the community. But this, of course, split the community on this issue. This writer heard one of the governor's supporters order a relative to abstain from the community demonstration, saying, "I don't want anyone of our family at the airport."

This is just one of the many examples of the divided power structure resulting from a vacuum in leadership in the Detroit community—a vacuum which reduces the community's influence and prestige.

Socio-economic Status

Income is higher in Toledo because of the occupational pattern: Detroit is a community of factory workers, while Toledo is a business community. However, the average income of both communities indicates that both have higher yearly incomes than the average American family, despite the fact that the members of both communities in general and of Toledo in particular tend to understate their yearly income as a natural precaution against being caught reporting higher than they probably did for income tax purposes. In fact, this question of total family income was the most difficult one on which to obtain a response; it was such a cause of suspicion that some respondents refused to cooperate in completing the interview.

The average family income in both communities is $6,987.50, in contrast to $5,966 for all families in the United States in 1954.[13] Even when we compare it with the $6,297 average of nonfarm families, the average family income in both communities still exceeds it. In Toledo the average family income is $8,269. In contrast, the average family income in the Detroit community is $5,706, which is much closer to the average income of all American families.

This high income level in both communities enables the majority of the families to own their homes. In the two communities combined, 75 per cent own their homes. These homes are equivalent to those of the American middle class. There is at least one vacuum cleaner and a refrigerator in every household. The great

[13] *The Economic Almanac* (New York, 1958), p. 350.

majority in both communities have a radio, television set, telephone, and washing machine; 80 per cent own cars. On Sundays in Toledo, there is hardly enough parking space in the street to accommodate the cars in which the members drive their children to Sunday school and prayer.

Islam, in fact, emphasizes building a better charitable life as a means both to itself and the ultimate happiness in the Hereafter. It encourages its followers to fully participate in life and to acquire wealth through legal and moral means. Simultaneously, it warns its followers not to abuse their wealth. The better a man to mankind, the closer he is to God and the wealthier he will become. In Islam, good relations with God are associated with wealth in this life in addition to happiness in the life after: "Seek the pardon of your Lord. Lo! He was even forgiving. He will let loose the sky for you in plenteous rain. And will help you with wealth and sons, and will assign unto you gardens and will assign unto you rivers."[14]

Relations with the Old Countries

The relations of the Arab Moslems in America with the old countries are still strong. The first-generation immigrants often send money home to support their closest relatives. When they go for visits, they contribute money to build homes, hospitals, and schools in their original villages. The degree of economic importance of the Arab emigrants became obvious recently in the Arab world when, according to the Cairo newspaper, *Al-Ahram*,

> The executive committee for Arab Emigrants' Affairs in Damascus prepared a program designed to ensure cooperation between Arab emigrants residing abroad and the United Arab Republic . . . Three sub-committees [were] formed to study the possibility of employing Arab emigrants to the U. S. or Americans of Arab descent as technical experts in the United Arab Republic and to promote cultural exchanges between the emigrants and the U.A.R.
>
> Another question under consideration is the possibility of employing emigrants' capital in various development projects. The number of Americans of Arab descent in the United States is estimated at 700,000.[15]

[14] *Qur'an*, Noah, LXXI, 10-12.

[15] *News of the United Arab Republic* (Washington, August 1959), Vol. 10, No. 8, p. 4. This is in accordance to our estimate in this book, since the Arab Moslems (78,000) represent ten per cent of the Arab Christians.

This new official concern for the Arab emigrants and their descendants will eliminate the old complaint that the emigrants are ignored by the old countries. The Arab-Americans feel that they have contributed much to their former countries, as well as to the Arab cause in America, but that this has not been appreciated by the Arab states. They complain that sometimes they have been victims of their generosity. They report, for example, that during and after the Palestine War, many Arabs came to these communities and collected large amounts of money, a great deal of which was never used for the purpose for which it was solicited. Some officials of Arab states were very generously welcomed by prominent members of the Arab communities here, but when these Arab-Americans visited Arab countries they were ignored by those officials whom they had welcomed. Such unequal treatment lessened the Americans' concern for the Arab countries. But the recent change in official attitude of the Arab governments toward the Arab-Americans promises to improve relations. The reaction of the Arab-Americans is favorable to this plan to encourage them to visit the Arab world.[16]

Thirty-six per cent of the Arab-Americans in Toledo and Detroit have visited their countries of origin at least once. The purposes of the trips varied: business, education, settling down there, and marriage, as shown in Table 8. Most of those who returned to their original country went for a visit, probably for nostalgic reasons or to show how well off they had become in America. Whatever the reason, most of those who went back felt at home in their native country but wanted to return to America (Table 9).

According to Table 9, 81 per cent of those who returned to their native country desired to come back to the United States after concrete experiences that enabled them to compare their country of origin with that of adoption. This high percentage indicates a residential preference which psychologically enhances acculturation. This preference is accentuated by the response to the question "Would you want to spend the rest of your life here or back there?" Table 10 shows that 70.1 per cent said they wanted to settle here, against 15.6 per cent who expressed the desire for settling there in the native country.

[16] "Lebanon: Home Visit," in *Time*, August 3, 1959, pp. 26-27.

TABLE 8

Distribution of the Respondents Who Did and Did Not Return to the Original Country, and Their Reasons for Returning

		RETURNED TO NATIVE COUNTRY						
	Did Not Return	*Visit*	*Business*	*Education*	*Settling Down*	*To Get Married*	*Other*	*Total*
No.	270	78	4	2	31	21	16	422
%	64.0	18.5	1.0	0.5	7.3	5.0	3.7	100.0

TABLE 9

Distribution of Respondents' Feelings in Their Native Country

Feeling	No.	%
Felt at home, wanted to remain	28	18.4
Felt at home, but wanted to return to U. S.	77	50.7
Felt strange, but wanted to remain	1	0.7
Felt strange, wanted to return to U. S.	46	30.2
Total	152	100.0

In general, one can sense the difference between the two communities in their orientation and affection toward the Arab countries. The Toledo community is oriented to think of the Arab countries as mainly Moslem, in a religious sense. Thus its affection toward the Middle East is held through religious ties. The Detroit community thinks of the Middle East as equally Arab and Moslem, but it is more receptive to the Arab nationalistic appeal.

Political Views

The "Syrians" in America today, including the Moslems, differ in many ways from those who had no political aspiration when Professor Hitti wrote about them more than forty years ago.[17]

TABLE 10

Distribution of the Sample on Country Preference

Country Preference	No.	%
Old Country, unconditional	66	15.6
Old Country, but Hindered by Children or Business	19	4.5
Old Country, if Economic Conditions Improve There	15	3.6
America	296	70.1
No Definite Feeling	26	6.2
Total	422	100.0

[17] Philip K. Hitti, *The Syrians in America* (New York, 1924), p. 89.

Today, political interests are high in the two Moslem communities of Detroit and Toledo. Due to the size of the Detroit community, the politicians as well as trade union leaders seek its support. During the field research, there was a dispute between the mayor of Dearborn and the fire-police union over an economic issue whose resolution called for a county vote. Both sides in the dispute sought the support of the Detroit Moslem community through its leaders. The community asked both sides in the dispute to send representatives to explain their views, following which the community leaders recommended how the Moslems should vote. On a higher political level, the governor of Michigan does not miscalculate the heavy collective weight of the Detroit Arab community.

The Federation of Islamic Associations

The formal Islamic movement in America is associated with the political awakening of Arabs resulting from events that took place in this country and in the Arab World. The movement was inspired, first, to achieve equal recognition for the American Moslems. "While in service during World War II, Abdallah Igram [a second-generation member and the Federation's first president] recognized a lack of information and misinterpretation of the tenets of Islam, the second largest monotheistic faith in the world. As a solution to the problem, he envisioned an organization that would achieve equal recognition for the American Muslim."[18]

Having fought in the two World Wars in the American armed forces, the Moslems sought religious recognition in the Army. Concerning faith, they were listed in the residual category. The Moslem soldier was given an X identification. It is not surprising, therefore, that the Islamic movement was started in the American army by a second-generation officer.

The Palestine War

But why, if the dubious status of the Moslems in the American army was felt and resented for so long, was this movement delayed until 1952? It is said that the Palestinian War in which the Arab countries were defeated awakened the nationalistic sentiments of the Arab-Americans in general and especially of the

[18] From a pamphlet titled "The Federation of Islamic Associations in the United States and Canada" (Washington, D.C.: The Islamic Center, n.d.).

Moslems. It is not surprising that the soldier, Mr. Igram, felt the humiliation as expressed by the third president of the Federation: "The Palestinian War humiliated every Arab in America." The Moslems here believed America to be the leader of the international conspiracy against the countries of their faith. The Palestinian War and the creation of Israel with Western and American aid caused among Moslems here an ambivalent attitude; their loyalty to America was weakened by their resentment against its political role in the Middle East and by their disappointment over the defeat of the Arab states in Palestine. Thus the Palestinian War accelerated the Islamic movement in America.

The Role of the Egyptian Revolution in the Islamic Movement in America

The Islamic movement in America, though not initiated by the Egyptian Revolution, was stimulated by it. The lag between the defeat of the Arab countries, which resulted in 1948 in the existence of Israel, and the official creation of the Islamic Federation in 1952 (it was first called "The International Muslim Society") was a period of gestation. The first convention was held in Cedar Rapids, Iowa, attended by more than 400 Moslems, and on June 28, 1952, the International Muslim Society was created, less than one month before the Egyptian Revolution took place. In fact, both movements had one common factor: the Palestinian War, which shook the Arabs in the homeland and abroad. The organization might have failed as many others have, had it not been for the electric effect of the Egyptian Revolution which stimulated Arab nationalist pride in America as well as the Middle East.

Despite its survival, in contrast to preceding efforts, the Islamic Federation's activities up to now have been minimal and, in fact, do not really involve anything worth mentioning except an annual convention. One Toledo respondent complains that this annual gathering itself seems to be mainly for dancing and singing. Another prominent person in the Detroit community described the 1959 annual convention as "successful in collecting money, but very weak and disappointing in other respects." In the two communities and surrounding areas, the Islamic Federation has no regular activities at all, nor does it enjoy a strong reputation. The third president of the Federation lives in Toledo, but is not an active member of its Moslem community. The Islamic Federation has little information about the Moslems in America and had no official headquarters up to the time of this research. Its written constitution states: "As an expression of their obligations and services in the path of God, the Moslems in the United States and Canada shall organize themselves under the present constitution to promote and teach the spirit, ethics, philosophy, and culture of Islam among themselves and their children."[19] Throughout its fourteen years thus far, the Islamic Federation has not fulfilled these tenets. Another goal is to "establish close contacts with all parts of the Moslem World and participate in the modern renaissance of Islam."[20] To achieve this goal, the Federation in 1959 established formal relations with the United Arab Republic. President Nasser invited the third and previous presidents of the Federation to visit Egypt, and contributed $44,000 for building a second Islamic center in Detroit to be the Islamic Federation's headquarters.[21]

Arab Nationalism

We can see that political consciousness of the Moslems in America is a very recent development associated with the political events in the homeland since 1948. The Arab defeat in the Palestinian War aroused the anger of Moslems in America but discouraged them as well. The Egyptian Revolution and the rise of President Nasser to world prominence, however, aroused their sense of nationalism. To Moslems in America as well as in the Middle East, Nasser became the symbol of Arab nationalism. In almost every Moslem home in America there is more than one picture of Nasser. In their social and religious events, the Moslems receive enthusiastically and applaud strongly the songs about Nasser. As a prominent woman in Detroit put it to a Jordanian official accompanying King Hussein during his visit in 1959: "Whenever a party is opened in the name of the Prophet, no one is particularly moved. If it is opened in the name of God, no one cares either. But the name of Gamal Abdel-Nasser electrifies the hall." This is no exaggeration. The Moslems have great faith and trust in Nasser and under his personal leadership they seek the unification of the Arab countries.

[19] See the Constitution of the Islamic Federation in Appendix, pp. 153-60.
[20] *Ibid.*
[21] *New York Times*, Section 1, p. 21, September 20, 1959; *Al-Ahram*, Cairo, p. 7, September 11, 1959.

The Arabs in America feel a common cultural, religious, and linguistic bond, in addition to the geographical and historical connection, with the Arab countries. But these links are not the immediate source of either Arab nationalistic feeling or Islamic movement in America. The immediate factors are the continuing threat posed by the existence of Israel and Nasser's resistance to Israel and the Western political pressure. American Moslems are proud of Nasser as "the first Arab leader" who dared to say "No" to the Western Powers, and even challenged them by nationalizing the Suez Canal. It was said that at the time of the 1956 attack upon Egypt, the price of the short-wave radios in Toledo and Detroit went up. A great majority of the Moslem families bought one. Following the news from Egypt, the two communities were gathered in groups around their radios and when the invasion was over, both communities contributed money for the victims of Port Sa'id. The demonstration by the Detroit community against King Hussein protested his hostile policy toward President Nasser; this was another example of the political consciousness of this community toward the current political issues in the homeland. The investigator had the chance to observe that reception. He had another chance to observe a third example of the nationalistic spirit. On Algeria Day, the Detroit community called for a party at which $1,400 was raised and sent to the Algerian fighters via President Nasser.

All these nationalistic activities, initiated and performed by the Arab Moslems, strengthen the Islamic movement in America and increase the friendly relations between the Moslems in America and the Arab countries. The Islamic Federation may become the means by which such a development will take place. But the relations between the Moslem communities in America and in the Middle East will be very much affected by the degree of religiosity as well as of assimilation in the American communities.

CHAPTER THREE

Assimilation

It is not a simple matter to measure and establish a scale of assimilation. Being acculturated and assimilated involves changes in values and attitudes as well as in personal opinions, and objective questions may not always reach the subtleties of these changes.

The Scale's Components

There were nine questions in the interview schedule designed to measure the degree of the respondent's assimilation into the American culture. These questions dealt with two aspects: one's values and outlook on life, and one's views on the adopted society (America) as well as one's station in and affection toward it.

The first four of the following nine components deal with the first aspect, while the remaining five deal with the second. These nine items are:

1. Religio-centrism or non-centrism.
2. Opinions about predestination.
3. Opinions about traditional customs.
4. Attitudes toward mixed religious marriage.
5. Preferred country of residence.
6. How respondents feel Americans consider them.
7. How respondents consider themselves.
8. How respondents compare Arabs with Americans.
9. Language used in conversation at home.

The degree of association of these nine items was found to be .60 of the uncorrected tetrachoric correlation. The following questions treat the above-mentioned items respectively.

The question concerning the first item asks: "After the spread of Islam, would you say that (1) Islam is the *only* religion accepted by God; (2) Christianity and Judaism are as accepted as Islam; (3) or something else?" The responses to this question were grouped into four categories, as shown in Table 11. As the

TABLE 11

Distribution of Respondents on Religion's Acceptance

	No.	%	Score
1. God accepts *only* Islam	100	23.7	
2. God accepts Christianity and Judaism as well	258	61.1	1
3. Every religion is accepted	61	14.5	
4. Do not know	3	.7	
Total	422	100.0	

responses to every item of the nine questions were dichotomized for the simple scoring method, affirmative responses to answers 2 and 3 were taken as a positive sign of assimilation into the American religious values and scored 1 as against 0 for the affirmative answers to questions 1 and 4.

The responses to the question "Do you agree or not that God predestined everyone's future?" were grouped into four categories, as shown in Table 12. This table shows that 65.4 per cent are traditionalistic and believe in predestination. Since the American culture, as well as true Islam, stresses the principle of "free will," answers 2, 3, and 4 were taken as positive signs of assimilation and scored 1; answer 1 was a sign of traditionalism and scored 0.

The question dealing with item 3 asks: "In your personal opinion, should a good Moslem woman in America be veiled or not?" There were three categories of response to this question, as shown in Table 13. It is very surprising that 43 per cent still hold the traditionalistic view that women should wear veils. In fact, the majority of the Shi'ah women in both communities practice the tradition of wearing veils, in the sense that they cover their hair, arms, and legs, but not their faces—as the phrase "wearing a

TABLE 12

Distribution of Respondents on Predestination

	No.	%	Score
1. Agree	276	65.4	
2. Unsure	85	20.1	
3. Disagree	40	9.5	1
4. Do not know	21	5.0	
Total	422	100.0	

TABLE 13

Distribution of Respondents on Whether American Moslem Women Should Wear a Veil

	No.	%	Score
1. Should	181	43	
2. Should not	223	53	1
3. No opinion	18	4	1
Total	422	100	

veil" might imply. Answers 2 and 3 were taken as positive signs of assimilation and scored 1; answer 1 was taken as a sign of traditionalism and scored 0.

The question on mixed marriage asks: "Suppose a Moslem girl fell in love with a Christian boy and wanted to marry him. What do you think her parents should do?" The responses to this question were grouped into seven categories, as shown in Table 14. Since marriage in America is considered a personal matter, answers 5, 6, and 7 were taken as positive signs of assimilation. But since the Catholics have a particular attitude concerning the children—to obtain a degree of homogeneity without infringing on the personal freedom of the spouse's action, they require that the offspring be of their faith—answer 4 was added to 5, 6, and 7 and all scored 1; answers 1, 2, and 3 scored 0.

The responses to the question "Would you want to spend the rest of your life here or in your native country?" were grouped into five categories in Table 15. Those who wanted to spend the

TABLE 14

Distribution of Respondents on a Moslem Girl Wanting to Marry a Christian Boy

	No.	%	Score
1. By all means, try to prevent marriage	91	21.6	
2. Allow only if boy becomes Moslem	60	14.2	
3. Advise her not to marry him	106	25.1	
4. Allow on condition that children become Moslem	60	14.2	1
5. Not interfere	59	14.0	1
6. Be indifferent	43	10.2	1
7. Do not know	3	.7	1
Total	422	100.0	

TABLE 15

Distribution of Respondents on Which Country Is More Desirable

	No.	%	Score
1. Old country	66	15.6	
2. Old country, but children or business prevent return	19	4.5	
3. Old country, if economic situation there improves	15	3.6	
4. America	296	70.1}	1
5. No definite feeling	26	6.2	
Total	422	100.0	

rest of their lives in America showed a positive sign of assimilation and scored 1.

Item 6 asks: "In general, do you feel that the Americans here consider you an American, or an Arab, or both?" The responses to this question were grouped into four categories, shown in Table 16. Answer 2 was taken as a positive sign and scored 1.

The responses to the question "What do you consider yourself?" were also grouped into four categories, shown in Table 17. Answer 2 was also taken as a positive sign of assimilation and scored 1.

TABLE 16

How Respondents Feel Americans Consider Them

	No.	%	Score
1. Arab	109	25.8	
2. American	132	31.3}	1
3. Both	168	39.8	
4. No definite feeling	13	3.1	
Total	422	100.0	

TABLE 17

What Respondents Consider Themselves

	No.	%	Score
1. Arab	136	32.2	
2. American	107	25.4}	1
3. Both	171	40.5	
4. No definite feeling	8	1.9	
Total	422	100.0	

TABLE 18

How Respondents Compare Arabs with Americans in Fairness of Social Relations

	No.	%	Score
1. The Arabs as fair	132	31.3}	1
2. The Arabs more fair	135	32.0	
3. The Arabs less fair	129	30.6}	1
4. Do not know	26	6.1}	
Total	422	100.0	

The question concerning item 8 asks: "Compared with the Americans as a whole, do you think that the Arabs are as fair, more fair, or less fair in their social relations?" The responses to this question were grouped into four categories, shown in Table 18. Answers 1, 3, and 4 indicate non-ethnocentrism and were thus taken as positive signs of assimilation and scored 1.

The last question asks: "In general, would you say that you use Arabic in your conversation at home (1) always; (2) often; (3) seldom; or (4) never." The responses to this question were grouped into four categories, as shown in Table 19. As language is an indicator of assimilation, answers 3 and 4 were taken as positive signs and scored 1.

Intercorrelation of Items

The first question is whether these nine items have anything in common, that is, whether they seem to measure a single variable; this variable we infer from the content to be the intensity of assimilation into American society. Since we dichotomize all questions, either positive or negative, a correlation measure for a 2 × 2 table had to be selected, and a high degree of correlation was obtained and justified the usage of these items as components of the assimilation scale.

TABLE 19

How Often Respondents Use Arabic at Home

	No.	%	Score
1. Always	104	24.6	
2. Often	82	19.4	
3. Seldom	127	30.0}	1
4. Never	109	26.0}	
Total	422	100.0	

Assimilation in the Scheme of the Two Communities

The difference between the Toledo and Detroit communities on the scale of assimilation is found to be significant at a level of .01. The significant difference between the two communities occurs in the high and low classes on the assimilation scale, as shown in Table 20. The Toledo community compared with Detroit has a higher proportion on the high class of assimilation, 42 per cent as against 33 per cent, and a correspondingly lower proportion on the low class of assimilation, 17 per cent as against 25 per cent. Both communities are almost equal on the middle class.

The Nature of the Settlers in Each Community

Despite the similarity in background of the two communities, the members of the Detroit community, unlike those in Toledo, came from the old country directly to Detroit, where they established their ghetto-like colony in Dearborn. The conservative views along with the old traditional customs are preserved and still maintained to a great extent. One cannot but observe the Arabic atmosphere on Dix Street: here are many coffee-houses whose patrons speak Arabic and drink the same strong tea and Turkish coffee in small cups that they drank in the old country and play the same games. In almost every home the same Arabic food, such as the favorite Syrian dish of *Kebba Nayya* (raw ground lamb), is served. The Syrian groceries import food from Syria. The Syrian bakeries and pastry shops provide familiar foods too. It is not only externals that are the same: the family structure itself is unchanged, except where the second- or third-generation member has rebelled against exploitation by the extended family and moved away to be economically and personally independent.

TABLE 20

Differences between Toledo and Detroit on Assimilation Scale

Class of Assimilation	*Toledo* No.	*Toledo* %	*Detroit* No.	*Detroit* %
High	88	42	69	33
Middle	86	41	88	42
Low	37	17	54	25
Total	211	100	211	100

In contrast, the majority of the Toledo Moslems established their community after several years of peddling from one state to another. During that mobile transition period between leaving the old country and settling permanently in Toledo, they acquired the newer views of the socio-economic middle class. They lost some of the traditional tastes and values and came to admire American traits. "God bless America" is a common expression among these women when they compare life in America with their memories of the difficult life they left behind.

While the first-generation members of the Detroit community are aggressive in their Moslem loyalty and live on the margin of the American culture, the first-generation members of the Toledo community are moderate about their Moslem attachment and are part of American culture. They live in American homes and cook American food. The family structure has the American style of equality between the two spouses and the emphasis on making children happy. The old patriarchal family structure is changing to an equalitarian one as a result of the new economic and social roles played by the Moslem women in the Toledo community.

Ecological Factors and Occupation

The concentration of the great majority of the Detroit Moslems in the ghetto-like area in Dearborn is another barrier to assimilation. This concentration is due to the prevailing occupational pattern: most are laborers in the auto factories. The occupational pattern is itself a hindrance to assimilation, for unskilled or semi-skilled workers do not need high training. Moreover, since technological changes, especially automation, cut down communication, Moslem workers have had little need and opportunity to learn English on the job. They speak Arabic at home. The service at the mosque is delivered in Arabic (which has alienated the younger generation), and discussion in the social clubs or coffee-houses is also carried out in Arabic. The group lacks the conception of a great deal of the American culture because they do not have the terms to carry such conceptions.

Because of its concentration of a homogeneous group with identical ethnic background and distinct social customs, the Detroit community may justifiably be called a colony which is, perhaps, discriminated against by the middle and higher American socio-economic classes. It is not correct, however, to call the Toledo community a colony, for it lacks the spatial concentration.

The population of the Toledo community is randomly distributed throughout the city. The gathering of three or four families in one section does not indicate more than chance. As in Detroit, the residential pattern of the community is related to the occupational distribution. The majority of the Toledo Moslems are engaged in business, mainly bars and liquor-licensed restaurants, and are chiefly managers and owners. As the business places are evenly distributed all over the city, the natural desire to live closer to one's place of business also worked out to scatter the Moslems throughout the city. In their business as well as in their living they interweave with the Americans. Business and success depend to a large degree on skill in conversation and communication in English. Table 21 shows the difference in percentage between the two communities in labor and business occupations in general.

Income

Whether or not income may be regarded as a function of assimilation, it is at least associated with it. The stress of the American culture on material success has stirred the economic motivation of the immigrants. In this respect, the Toledo community has achieved a higher degree of assimilation. In pursuit of materialistic success, it has sacrificed some of its religious values by trading in liquor; this kind of religious deviation in occupation is a sizeable measure of assimilation. Table 22 shows the difference in income distribution between the two communities in their lower and higher levels of yearly income.

The table also shows the relation between assimilation and economic achievement. The relatively high degree of assimilation of the Toledo community resulted from the entire integration with the rest of the city, through which a harmony between different values in the two cultures was brought about. Though the American success pattern has prevailed over the traditionalistic Moslem religious values, the liquor dealers of the Toledo com-

TABLE 21

Labor and Business by the Two Communities

Community	*Business*	*Labor*
Toledo	62	40
Detroit	38	60
Total	100	100

TABLE 22

Lower and Higher Yearly Income by the Two Communities

Area	*Less than $4,000*	*$9,000 plus*
Toledo	43	69
Detroit	57	31
Total	100	100

munity do preserve the values to some extent, by admitting that drinking alcohol is forbidden and by abstaining from drink. They obeyed the explicit Quranic prohibition to drink, but evaded the prophetic prohibition to trade in liquor when they found it profitable. Between that kind of personal obedience and occupational practice exists a gap of secular rationalization. They claim that liquor stores and bar licenses exist almost everywhere in America. "If we don't sell liquor, someone else will anyway," they say. "We neither encourage drink nor initiate drinking places. Drinking is a habit in this country and we just followed the pattern as any legal occupation. Furthermore," they add, "our customers are not Moslems, they are Americans. We scorn any Moslem who may come to drink." This kind of secular rationalization is what is meant by a harmony between two different sets of values, accelerating the process of assimilation in the Toledo community without unnecessary cultural shock of serious deviation or, at least, without psychological repercussions.

Another factor in assimilation is the energetic pattern of the members of the Toledo community, as represented by this case history.

A Case Study in Toledo

The people of the Toledo community are business-minded. Sam (Americanized from Sami) Othman's life history may be a good representation of the pattern of economic striving in his community.

Sam came to America in 1912 when he was 13 years old, with eight friends from Qada Rashayya, Lebanon. His father, who had made three trips to America before Sam's birth, gave him his conception of America. He was the only Moslem on the boat to America. The immigration officers did not allow him to land, so he had to go back on the same boat, landing in England. He had a countryman in Cincinnati whose name was Hidar. Hidar wanted Sam to work for him, so he sent Sam $50 and asked him to return to America under another name. He wrote to Sam instructing him to tell the immigration officers that he was going to his brother, Kamil Hidar, to study in America. Sam arrived in Philadelphia under the name of Joseph Hidar and was admitted.

Like most Arab Moslem immigrants to America, Sam was a farmer from a lower socio-economic class family. Table 23 shows the percentages of the respondents' occupational distribution in the old country. The 34 per cent in the first category represent the females and those immigrants who left the old country when they were very young. It is justified to add them to the second category and consider both as representing farming family backgrounds. We may say, then, that 81 per cent of the Arab Moslem immigrants of these two communities were from farming families. This conforms with the general pattern of early immigration to this country from eastern and southern Europe in the nineteenth and early twentieth centuries.[1]

Knowing no English, Sam followed the occupational pattern of the majority of the Arab immigrants: peddling dry goods from house to house. Table 24 shows the distribution, in percentage, of the first occupations of the first-generation respondents. The results follow the general occupational pattern among many other ethnic groups.

The majority of the immigrants came to America with neither enough capital nor adequate skills. Peddling does not require

TABLE 23

Occupations of the First-Generation Respondents in the Old Country

	No.	%
1. Not employed	50	34
2. Farmer	69	47
3. Unskilled	6	4
4. Skilled	4	3
5. Clerical	4	3
6. Professional	3	2
7. Business	3	2
8. Student	7	5
Total	146	100

[1] See William Isaac Thomas and Florjan Znanieki, *The Polish Peasant in Europe and America* (2 Vols., New York, 1927).

TABLE 24

First-Generation Respondents' First Occupations in America

	No.	%
1. Peddlers	58	40
2. Salesmen	13	9
3. Business	12	8
4. Unskilled	28	19
5. Working with relatives	31	21
6. Farmers	4	3
Total	146	100

capital. The early Jewish merchants discovered and utilized the business potential of the Syrians. They found them patient and eager to bear hardships to earn money and thus they supplied them with goods. The Arabs in general and the Arab Moslems in particular had known peddling before and after the rise of Islam. In fact, the diffusion of Arabic and Islamic cultures to many continents and nations owed a great deal to the traders. Islam has been and still is diffused throughout Asia and Africa by these people's ancestors who carried the Islamic values and Arabic customs along with their goods from nation to nation. In turn, the receptivity of these traders led them to bring back to Islam different values and cultural elements. The four Islamic jurisprudential schools give ample evidence of the cultural reciprocity which nourished early Islamic thoughts in theology, philosophy and literature. From the viewpoint of cultural diffusion, the anthropological approach may indeed yield fruitful results, should it be utilized for analysis of Islamic jurisprudence and comparative studies of the four jurisprudential schools.

Sam Othman peddled for fifteen years, earning money and learning American ways. His occupational and geographical mobility is typical of that of the Toledo community. After saving some money, he entered the Oriental rug business for three years. He managed to support himself and to send "home" about $3,000 to his mother and brothers. In addition, he saved $3,000 with which he became a partner with three Greeks in a restaurant in West Virginia. The business was run down but Sam managed to revive it and made it flourish; then he sold out his share and returned to peddling.

In the American environment, Sam had unpleasant experiences with the American girls, who, in his eyes, failed to reach the moral standard he wanted in a wife. Therefore, he returned to the old country after an absence of twenty-six years. His mother introduced him to an attractive Kurdish girl. He married her and built a home over there. In 1939, hearing of the war in Europe, he hastily left for America again. America entered the war and communication was cut off before he had a chance to bring his wife to America.

Sam peddled again for three months. Then he opened a luncheonette. He bought and sold several businesses, always dissatisfied with his partners, the locality, or the kind of business. He even went to work in the Ford plant in Dearborn but could not endure the restrictions of factory work. At length, he decided to return to the Middle East to bring back his wife. He remained a year, and in 1947 came back to America with his wife. He started a rug cleaning business in Ohio but this time he lost everything and was in debt $3,000. He borrowed $170 with which he and his wife entered a small business again. After three years they paid the $3,000 debt and managed to save $12,000. They went to Los Angeles to open a liquor store and in nine months they lost $6,000. Disappointed, they went to his wife's relatives in Toledo, where they rested for a year. Sam then resumed the pattern of buying and selling small businesses and then built a motel, which he sold at a great profit. He used part of this money to buy an apartment house, which still provides him a good, steady income. Now 67 years old, he is retired but is still restless and pines for the old buying and selling and moving about, despite the losses and uncertainties.

The Life Pattern of the Arab Moslems in America

Sam's life history is not unique. It is the general pattern of the economic struggle of the majority of the Arab Moslems in America who found themselves in strange social surroundings. Lacking both language and skill, the first-generation immigrants engaged either in unskilled labor or in peddling. Detroit's industrial activities attracted the Detroit Moslems and thus the occupational mobility in the Detroit community has not been as rapid as in the Toledo community. Factory labor also put a low ceiling on the process of assimilation in the Detroit community. Most of the first-generation immigrants who are now engaged in the auto industry started their careers in it. By encouraging concentration and isolation, the industrial character of the Detroit community helped the Moslems to preserve traditional values.

Among the first-generation immigrants in the Detroit community, 32 per cent still do not speak English, as against only 13 per cent in the Toledo community. Merchandising, peddling, and business pursuits helped to integrate the Toledo community with the American society. On the scale of assimilation we found only 17 per cent of the Toledo community with low assimilation, against 25 per cent in the Detroit community, despite the fact that the latter community is older than the one in Toledo. The ratio of the first-generation immigrants to the second- and third-generation is much smaller in the Detroit community than in the Toledo community. The difference in occupational pattern between the two communities is correlated with the degree of assimilation in each.

Generational Differences

Though the Toledo business community has been cited as highly assimilated to the American culture, more so than the Detroit working community, there are significant intergenerational differences within each community. As among other ethnic groups, assimilation becomes easier for each succeeding generation, as shown in Table 25. There is a sharp jump between the first and second generation on the three classes of assimilation: 40 per cent of the first generation in both communities are still underassimilated, against 13 per cent of the second generation. Expressed positively, those who are highly assimilated to American culture comprise 11 per cent of the first generation in both communities and 48 per cent of the second generation.

Through the compulsory school system the second generation

TABLE 25
Assimilation, by Generation

Assimilation	Generation					
	First		*Second*		*Third*	
	No.	%	No.	%	No.	%
High	16	11	95	48	46	59
Middle	71	49	77	39	26	34
Low	59	40	27	13	5	7
Total	146	100	199	100	77	100

acquired naturally and without great effort the linguistic tool of culture. Through intimate contacts with their playmates and schoolmates, the second-generation members had the chance to compare two different cultures and ways of life. The unfavorable socio-economic conditions in the old countries at the time their parents came to America leave no doubt in the judgment of the second-generation members: they prefer the American socio-economic and political structure over that of the old country. In fact, they consider themselves luckier than their parents to have been born in this country. The parents share this view. The first-generation immigrants are proud to hear their children speaking English fluently like any American. It is also very common for the first-generation members to give their children American nicknames. In one family there are Mike, Ralph, Ronald, Fred, Dennis, Vicki, Stephen, and Churchill for outside identification, while the Arabic names are kept for the family and community identification.

The second generation plays a transitional role between the old and new cultures and thus is often the victim of both. The members of the second generation teach the members of the first generation a great deal about the American culture. But it is hard for the first-generation members, who are dominated by a patriarchal family image, to accept the reversal of roles which makes them pupils of their own children. This widens the cultural gap between the two generations. Most of the second-generation members, in response to the question, "About what things do you most frequently disagree with your father?" mention that their fathers are slow at making decisions and have a habit of arguing about little things. Among the common complaints against the mothers are that they "interfere" in their children's personal affairs, are too absorbed in the social life of the immigrant women, and engage in too much malicious gossip in the style of the old country.

The two generations therefore live in two different social atmospheres with separate outlooks on life. The first-generation members are affected by the memories of their great efforts to make their way in the strange land. Looking forward, they realize that socially as well as religiously they have lost their offspring to America as well as to Christianity. They admit that they have gained economic wealth but they doubt whether that wealth compensates for their loss. Nowadays, they do not advise any

Moslem to repeat their own fate. They are prisoners in two senses: they have acquired a new socio-economic status which they do not want to give up; and their American-born children do not share with them the desire to go back to the old country with the acquired wealth. The second-generation members see backwardness and misery in the old country and open opportunities and freedom in America.

Generational Differences between the Two Communities

The higher socio-economic status achieved by the Toledo community first-generation members plus the pattern of the ecological distribution of the community have created in the members a stronger attachment to American culture and values. This cultural appreciation by Toledo's first-generation Moslems has facilitated the process of assimilation. Table 26 shows the percentage distribution of the first generation in both communities on the scale of assimilation. Thirty-two per cent of the Toledo first generation are in the low class of assimilation, against 52 per cent of the Detroit first generation, while 14 per cent of the Toledo first generation, against 6 per cent in Detroit, are in the high class of assimilation. The difference between the first generations in the two communities is significant at a level of .01. This difference, as indicated in the general patterns of the two communities, is somehow related to the differing ecological patterns of industrial Detroit and commercial Toledo.

The degree of assimilation among the first generation in each community affects the degree of assimilation of the second generation. The Toledo second generation is found to be higher than the Detroit second generation on the scale of assimilation, as shown in Table 27. Seven per cent of the Toledo second generation, as against 20 per cent of the Detroit second generation, are underassimilated, while 54 per cent of the Toledo community,

TABLE 26

Assimilation by the First Generation in Both Communities

Community		*Low*	*Middle*	*High*	*Total*
Toledo	No.	28	46	12	86
	%	32	54	14	100
Detroit	No.	31	25	4	60
	%	52	42	6	100

TABLE 27

Assimilation by the Second Generation in Both Communities

Community		*Low*	*Middle*	*High*	*Total*
Toledo	No.	7	38	52	97
	%	7	39	54	100
Detroit	No.	20	39	43	102
	%	20	38	42	100

against 42 per cent of the Detroit second generation, are in the highest assimilation class. However, the rate of movement of the process of assimilation from the first to the second generation is almost twice as great in Toledo as it is in Detroit. This is shown by the following formula:

$$\frac{20}{52} \Big/ \frac{7}{32}$$

It means, in terms of generation, that the Toledo community is more advanced in assimilation than the Detroit community by one generation. In fact, the Toledo second generation resembles the Detroit third generation on the scale of assimilation, as shown in Table 28.

The difference between the Toledo second generation and the Detroit third generation on the scale of assimilation is negligible. The moderate attitudes of the Toledo first-generation members accelerated the process of assimilation among their children, while the traditional timid attitudes of the Detroit first-generation members hindered the flow of assimilation among the Detroit second generation. The Detroit second-generation members, in general, are apathetic, seeing the persistence of the old generation's grasp on the leadership of the community's affairs. In the

TABLE 28

Assimilation by Toledo Second Generation and Detroit Third Generation

Community		*Low*	*Middle*	*High*	*Total*
Toledo 2nd	No.	7	38	52	97
	%	7	39	54	100
Detroit 3rd	No.	3	24	22	49
	%	6	49	45	100

Toledo community, social and religious leadership is left to the second-generation members.

The Toledo second generation has played a transitional role by (1) Americanizing traditional patterns which it handed down to the third generation, and (2) permitting the third generation to adopt its own American values, which then increased the level of assimilation of the entire community irrespective of generational differences. Moreover, the second generation has learned certain American forms from the third, playing bridge, for example, which it has then transmitted back to the first. Thus the second generation is a channel through which the first and third have an impact on each other.

In Detroit, however, the Americanization of the third generation has left the first unaffected because the second generation, hardly assimilated, has lost contact with both the first and third. Thus there is a sharp departure in assimilation between the third and second generation in the Detroit community; in Toledo, the process of assimilation has worked its way smoothly without noticeable difference from the second to the third generation. This smooth transition in Toledo is the result of the second generation's adjustment to the American culture. There is, however, one difference between these two generations: 86 per cent of the Toledo third generation are in the highest assimilation class, as against only 54 per cent of the Toledo second generation. But the corresponding difference between the Detroit third and second generations is much smaller: 45 per cent to 42 per cent. The similarity between the Detroit third and second generations is in the first and second classes of assimilation. But in the third class of assimilation are 6 per cent of the Detroit third generation, as against 20 per cent of the Detroit second generation. The following table shows the assimilation classes in both communities by the third and second generation.

As Table 29 shows, within three generations the assimilation process has worked its natural way but with different rates in the two communities. Both communities have about the same proportion of members in the third generation who fail to become more assimilated: 7 per cent in Toledo and 6 per cent in Detroit remain in the least assimilated class. Though there are no comparable data concerning this least assimilated residue among other ethnic groups, our finding conforms to general findings, which point to growing assimilation from the first to later generations. The de-

TABLE 29
Assimilation by the Second and Third Generations of Both Communities

Community		*Low*		*Middle*		*High*	
		2nd	3rd	2nd	3rd	2nd	3rd
Toledo	No.	7	2	38	2	52	24
	%	7	7	39	7	54	86
Detroit	No.	20	3	39	24	43	22
	%	20	6	38	49	42	45

gree of assimilation depends on the degree of exposure to the host culture. For this reason, the Toledo second generation has reached the same degree of assimilation as that of the Detroit third generation. And the third generation in both communities has reached a high degree of assimilation.

ASSIMILATION AND RELIGION

Acting in and interacting with an alien culture, the individual personality as well as the ethnic group tends to internalize the strange new values prevailing in the adopted society. New attitudes, which may or may not conflict with traditional norms, are developed toward the new prevailing values and thus the personality or the ethnic group is said to be within a certain social distance from the adopted culture. This distance from the adopted culture is the measurement of assimilation used in this study. The shorter the distance between an ethnic group and the new sets of values, the more assimilated is the group with regard to the adopted culture.

But there are certain elements in particular cultures that tend to hinder the process of assimilation of particular ethnic groups to any other culture. One of the strongest of these elements is religion. When religion is identical with nationality or race it tends to strengthen the group solidarity and thus weaken the process of its assimilation with the adopted culture. Mears has observed that Greece, dominated for four centuries by the Turks, centered its own concept of nationality about the Greek Orthodox Church.[2] Several centuries of Arab domination could not ab-

[2] Eliot Grinnell Mears, *Greece Today* (Stanford, 1929), p. 230.

sorb Spanish Christianity, religion being the main factor which preserved the national solidarity of Spain. Judaism has also served to solidify the group not only as a symbol of religious identification but of national and ethnic identification as well. The literature of minority groups provides ample evidence of the dysfunctional role that religion plays in the processes of assimilation and acculturation.

Dealing with our two Moslem communities within the assimilation frame of reference there are two questions to ask: (1) To what extent is Islam, as a religion, eufunctional in strengthening the ethnic identification of these two communities and consequently weakening the process of assimilation? (2) If there is a difference between the two communities in their degree of assimilation, should we not expect a negative correlation between assimilation and religiosity, that is, the more assimilated to the American culture the less religious a community is? This chapter deals with the first question, while the second is discussed in Chapter V.

As assimilation implies a change in the identification patterns, it permits minorities to absorb the dominant values in their own way and at their own speed. The dominant values in the American culture as seen by our two communities are materialistic. The early migration to the United States, as Warner and Srole have pointed out, resulted from forces of attraction exerted by the expanding American economy.[3] As Western peoples, with their stress on economic rationality, see a heaven with streets of gold,[4] the Moslem immigrants quickly adopted the dominant materialistic values which, indeed, attracted them to the new world. Our sample shows that 95 per cent of the first-generation immigrants were motivated to leave the old countries for America for economic reasons.

Having achieved economic success, the Moslems found themselves going through the process of what Daniel Glazer calls "reflexive conversion."[5] Their contact with the other ethnic and religious groups in America has widened the horizon of their

[3] W. Lloyd Warner and Leo Srole, *The Social Systems of American Ethnic Groups* (New Haven, 1945), p. 105.

[4] Thomas Ford Hoult, *The Sociology of Religion* (New York, 1958), p. 26.

[5] "Dynamics of Ethnic Identification," in *American Sociological Review*, Vol. 23, No. 1, February 1958, p. 33.

feelings toward mankind. Seventy-six per cent of our sample are found to be not religiocentric. They believe that Christianity and Judaism are religions as accepted as Islam in the sight of God. Sixty-two per cent of the sample believe that Americans are as fair as or more fair than Arabs in their social relations. In this respect, the Moslems are not ethnocentric. In the ethnic sense, the Arab Moslems in America are not very race conscious. Islam discourages in its believers the sense of ethnic monopoly based on national or race distinction. In this respect, Islam might very well be considered an assimilating religion in the broad terminological meaning of assimilation, which means dealing on a purely personal basis rather than on the basis of ethnic identification. The evidence of this statement is very clear in the basic Islamic sources as well as in literature. It is therefore justified to say that Islam, as a religion, is not altogether dysfunctional in the process of assimilation among our two communities.

Agents of Assimilation

The first agent of cultural assimilation is language. Without the new language the immigrant finds it difficult to understand, much less assimilate, the prevailing values in any given social system. A positively strong correlation is presumed between language and assimilation. The first immigrant males assimilate the adopted culture more rapidly than the females because the males, by means of interaction, learn the language sooner than the females. The language used at home in conversation is a reasonably precise indication for measuring the degree of assimilation. The sampling distribution of the two communities (Table 19) showed that, according to the linguistic criterion, 56 per cent have assimilated the American culture or at least possessed the necessary tool for assimilation.

Assimilation may also be measured in terms of preferred country of residence. Preference is a kind of evaluation which involves a certain degree of admiration or acceptance, which is conducive to, as well as indicative of, assimilation. The assimilated person would want to spend the rest of his life in the adopted country. As we saw in Table 15, 70 per cent have developed a sense of appreciation toward the American culture and may thus be considered assimilated.

Deserting traditional views shows the influence of adopting new values and a change in attitudes toward traditional customs. The veil, despite its decline in the urban areas of the Middle East, is still maintained in some rural areas from which the majority of the immigrants came. As Table 13 showed, 53 per cent have adopted the liberal views and can thus be considered positively assimilated. Also, the high degree of those still maintaining some old custom which is not currently maintained in the Middle East is very surprising. It is doubtful indeed that one could obtain today so high a proportion in favor of the veil even in the Middle East. It is a sign of preserving some traditionalistic views on old social customs while those customs have died off in the original countries.

Personal attitudes toward mixed religious marriage tend to become moderate whenever distance is obtained from the first generation. In their social interactions with the Americans, the Moslems in America have developed tolerant views concerning religious equality and they do not see a serious religious wrong in the mixed religious marriage. As we saw in Table 14, approximately two-fifths in the sample would not oppose intermarriage, provided, at least, that the Moslem spouse remains in the Islamic faith; 25 per cent have no condition beyond that. Fourteen per cent seem to favor an adaptation of Catholic practice by insisting that the children should be raised as Moslems. Another 14 per cent believe that the other partner should become Moslem. This is in conformity with the Islamic traditions. Forty-seven per cent are still strong in maintaining the traditionalistic religious attitude by strongly or moderately preventing the mixed religious marriage.

At the end of the assimilation scale of items come two which deal with the real question of identification—the core of assimilation. As Glazer has noted, the "experiences in America which make those who participate in them feel less than full Americans" hinder the process of assimilation.[6] These experiences shape the personality identification expressed from two aspects: (1) how one sees himself; and (2) how one sees himself through the eyes of the Americans. Thirty per cent of the Moslems of the two communities believe that the Americans consider them Americans, while 25 per cent consider themselves Americans (see Table 16).

[6] *Ibid.*

The Problem of Mixed Religious Marriage

The ratio of girls to boys among the Moslems of these two communities follows the present general pattern in America, that is, the number of girls slightly exceeds the number of boys. Besides, the Moslem boys, knowing their social as well as religious privilege, have the tendency to marry Americans. This tendency is nourished by the dating institution. It is acceptable for a Moslem boy to date an American girl, bring her home, and even introduce her to his family as his girl friend. It has not yet become fully accepted for a Moslem girl to act in a corresponding way. She is not supposed to date Americans. She may very well date Moslem boys. But since each community is composed of a few cohesive, related families, the affairs of all are quickly spread among them. As soon as a Moslem boy is seen with a Moslem girl, word spreads that he is engaged to her. Besides wanting to avoid this kind of gossip, the boy feels that he has to live up to what is expected of him morally as a good Moslem boy whose job is to protect the Moslem girl, who is also very likely a relative of his. The Moslem boy feels that with a Moslem girl he cannot have the freedom which he can enjoy with an American girl who is less restricted by her family and community. "They are dull dates," one interviewee frankly told the writer.

But the same accusation is made by the Moslem girls who are angry at the Syrian boys because of this conservative attitude. The Moslem girls in America feel oppressed by these traditional strains. In one of the monthly meetings of the Moslem Youth Organization held in Michigan City, Indiana, the writer had the chance to meet many youths from Toledo, Detroit, Michigan City, Chicago, and Canada. There was an informal discussion about the problems facing the youth in North America. Some thirty attractive young women of marriageable age almost monopolized the discussion, focusing on this problem of mixed marriage and the unequal religious strains put on them. "Why," they ask, "does Islam permit only men to marry non-Moslems?" Though they wanted equality in this respect, each was nevertheless unwilling to break the religious tradition by using the freedom provided by the American environment and taking this right for themselves.

It often happens that a father imports a relative of his from the old country with whom he shares his wealth to persuade him to marry his daughter. When quota limitations prevent such a plan, a Moslem from the Middle East is directed to come to America on a visitor's visa. He then goes to one of the Moslem communities in which he has many relatives and countrymen, and before his visa expires he marries a girl in the community and is able to remain in the United States. Few such marriages succeed, however; some only last long enough to enable the husband to become a citizen. The failure of such marriages results from the lack of a minimal homogeneity of cultural foreground and outlook, such as a common language and common social customs, to overcome the period of preadjustment. The Moslem girls in America do not look favorably upon such marriages. Those who accept them are among the least assimilated.

There is another solution to the mixed marriage. Many American boys are willing to convert to Islam in order to marry Moslem girls. But, though it is permitted by Islam, the Detroit community does not accept such an arrangement. A former director of the Islamic Center in Washington, D.C., was criticized in Detroit because he did not oppose that kind of marriage. "At the ceremony of marrying a Moslem girl to an American boy who converted to Islam," one woman complains, "he said before our girls that he would bless such a marriage. We don't like this. We don't want to lose our girls to the Americans." Thus they express their deep aversion to a mixed marriage, an aversion they find difficult to explain clearly. They do believe that such conversions are merely conveniences and not genuine ones. The rate of conversion to Christianity is higher in Detroit than in Toledo. It occurs mainly among the females. Because of this rigid attitude, it is associated with the mixed religious marriage. Knowing that she is socially outcast and that her future husband is not accepted as a full member in the community whether or not he has adopted Islam, the girl often breaks with her people. Socially, she needs religion for her children and in the surrounding open class society she finds Christianity open to her and to her children. In Toledo, on the other hand, the American husband finds himself easily affiliated with the Moslem community which absorbs him and his children.

Irrespective of one's attitude on the propriety of such marriages, there is no doubt that the mixed religious marriage in both communities is one of the strongest agencies of assimilation. But the mixed marriage, as an agency of assimilation, works differently in the two communities. In Detroit, the Moslem girl in a mixed marriage usually leaves the Moslem community entirely, so that her increased assimilation has little effect upon the assimilation of the Moslem community as a whole. In Toledo, however, the Moslem girl in a mixed marriage tends to retain her ties to the Moslem community and her personal assimilation becomes a means of increasing the entire community's level of assimilation. Within a short period of three generations, its effect in both communities is starting to appear. However, it is not obvious which is the cause and which the effect, that is, whether moderate attitudes toward the mixed religious marriage caused the higher degree of assimilation in that community or the other way around. We may merely assert, with a high degree of precision, the linear relations between the moderate attitudes observed in the Toledo community toward the mixed religious marriage and its high level on the scale of assimilation. To avoid a logical rejection of the above-mentioned statement, it is worth mentioning that the relation between assimilation and attitudes toward the mixed religious marriage is not based on the scale of assimilation and Item #6 which is one component of the scale itself. It is based on the scale of assimilation and the percentage of the mixed marriage in each community. Those counted are the mixed marriage cases *within* the community.[7]

The Sectarian Conflict in Both Communities

The role of Shi'ahs in each community may reveal further facts of assimilation. The Shi'ahs in America see the mosque structure as a Sunni institution. Therefore, they favor national clubs of a social kind rather than mosques.

Toledo

When the Toledo community raised money for a building in 1953, the Shi'ah members were in favor of constructing a national club. The majority of the community, however, voted for the mosque. After the mosque was erected in 1955, the Shi'ah members of the first generation quietly withdrew from the religious activities of the community. Not a single Shi'ah from the first generation attends the regular Friday Prayer or any other prayer

[7] There is no precise information on the great number of girls who left the Detroit community after being married to Americans.

TABLE 30

Assimilation Classes by the Two Communities Within the Three Generations

Area on Assimilation Classes		GENERATIONS 1st No.	1st %	1st *	2nd No.	2nd %	2nd *	3rd No.	3rd %	3rd *	Total No.	Total *	
Toledo	Low	28	19	31	7	3	8	2	3	2	37	41	91
Detroit		31	21	34	20	10	22	3	4	3	54	59	
Toledo	Middle	46	32	26	38	19	22	2	3	1	86	49	174
Detroit		25	17	14	39	20	23	24	31	14	88	51	
Toledo	High	12	8	8	52	26	34	24	31	15	88	57	157
Detroit		4	3	2	43	22	27	22	28	14	69	43	
Total of Generations		146	100		199	100		77	100		422		

* Percentage of each community on each class of assimilation.

TABLE 31

Test of Significance by χ^2

	Oij	eij	Oij–eij	(Oij–eij)²	$\frac{(Oij-eij)^2}{eij}$
37 × 146 = 5402/422	28	12.8	15.2	231	18.0
37 × 199 = 7363	7	11.4	–10.4	108	6.2
37 × 77 = 2849	2	6.8	– 4.8	23	3.4
54 × 146 = 7884	31	18.7	12.3	151	8.0
54 × 199 = 10746	20	25.5	– 5.5	30	1.1
54 × 77 = 4158	3	9.8	– 6.8	46	4.7
86 × 146 = 12556	46	29.8	16.2	262	8.8
86 × 199 = 17114	38	40.5	– 2.5	6	0.1
86 × 77 = 6622	2	15.7	–13.7	187	11.9
88 × 144 = 12848	25	30.4	–5.4	29	1.0
88 × 199 = 17512	39	41.5	– 2.5	6	0.1
88 × 77 = 6776	24	16.1	7.9	62	3.8
88 × 146 = 12848	12	30.4	–18.4	338	11.1
88 × 199 = 17512	52	41.5	10.5	110	2.6
88 × 77 = 6776	24	16.1	7.9	62	3.8
69 × 146 = 10074	4	23.9	–19.9	396	16.5
69 × 199 = 13731	43	32.5	10.5	110	3.3
69 × 77 = 5313	22	12.6	9.4	88	7.0
	422			χ^2	111.4

This exceeds the criterion of χ^2 (23.2) at a level of significance of .01. It shows that the difference between the two communities within the three generations on the scale of assimilation is very significant.

at the mosque, except on two special holy days; the religious festivals are also big social events. They participate in the other social events, such as when prominent personalities visit the community from Washington, D.C., or from the old countries. Despite their own ambivalence, they are content to see their children active in both social and religious activities of the mosque. They hope that the younger generation will know nothing of that sectarian conflict which still inhibits them.

This religious conflict between Shi'ahs and Sunnis in Toledo is not apparent on the surface. The Shi'ah first generation play no role in the religious affairs of the community, but support the mosque financially as a religious protection for their children. They are scattered in the city and thus sense a threat of Christianity which reminds them always that their children may be

TABLE 32

Assimilation Classes by Both Communities

Community		*Low*		*Middle*		*High*		*Total*	
		No.	%	No.	%	No.	%	No.	%
Toledo	No.	37		86		88		211	
	%		17		41		42		100
Detroit	No.	54		88		69		211	
	%		25		42		33		100
Total		91		174		157		422	

absorbed by another religion if that sectarian conflict is not checked at some point.

The depth of this conflict is great, as revealed in the activities of a Shi'ah leader, a Lebanese, who studied for several years at the Nagaf Institute in Iraq. This is one of the few religious schools for Shi'ahs. He came to America several years ago where he found the sectarian conflict dying in the Detroit community. He decided to revive it, chiefly, according to several respondents, as a means of increasing his own power. He encouraged the physical as well as the spiritual separation between the two sects in the Detroit community. Now the community has two separate religious institutions, the mosque for the Sunnis and the Arabian Hashimite Club for the Shi'ahs. The Shi'ahs in Detroit have ceased

TABLE 33

Test of Significance by χ^2

Oij	*eij*	*Oij–eij*	$(Oij\text{-}eij)^2$	$\frac{(Oij-eij)^2}{eij}$
88	78.5	9.5	90.25	1.2
86	87	–1.0	1.0	.0
37	45.5	–8.5	72.25	1.6
69	78.5	–9.5	90.25	1.2
88	87	1.0	1.0	.0
54	45.5	8.5	72.25	1.6
			χ^2	5.6

This is somehow shorter than the criterion of χ^2 at a level of significance of .05 (5.99). The difference is significant, however, at a level of .1, meaning that there is a significant difference between the two communities on the scale of assimilation.

TABLE 34
Scale of Assimilation by Generation

Generation	*High* No.	%	*Middle* No.	%	*Low* No.	%	*Total*
First	16	10	71	41	59	65	146
Second	95	60	77	44	27	30	199
Third	46	30	26	15	5	5	77
Total	157	100	174	100	91	100	422

	Oij	*eij*	*Oij–eij*	$(Oij-eij)^2$	$\frac{(Oij-eij)^2}{eij}$
146 × 157 = 22922/422	16	54.3	–38.3	1466	27.0
146 × 174 = 25404	71	60.2	10.8	116	1.9
146 × 91 = 13286	59	31.5	27.5	756	24.0
199 × 157 = 31243	95	74.0	21.0	441	5.9
199 × 174 = 34626	77	82.0	– 5.0	25	0.3
199 × 91 = 18109	27	42.9	–15.9	252	5.9
77 × 157 = 12089	46	28.6	17.4	302	10.5
77 × 194 = 13398	26	31.7	– 5.7	32	1.0
77 × 91 = 7007	5	16.6	–11.6	134	8.0
				χ^2	84.5

This greatly exceeds the χ^2 criterion (13.28) at a level of significance of .01. As is obvious, the correlation between generation and assimilation is positively strong. The strength of the correlation between assimilation and generation can be seen in terms of the contingency coefficient which is

$$C = \sqrt{\frac{84.5}{84.5 \quad 422}} = .41$$

This could be interpreted as a high correlation since the maximum value of C for a three-by-three table never reaches .80 (equivalent to r=1).

to participate in any religious activities with the Sunnis. Even those religious activities of a social nature, like the gathering for prayers at the two special Moslem festivals, are now separately maintained by each institution. This division has almost resulted in two separate denominations with completely distinct religious and social activities.

This sheikh aroused the criticism of the Shi'ahs in the Toledo community because he once tried publicly to stress the conflict at a very inopportune moment.

Detroit

The Shi'ah-Sunni conflict has been greater and more divisive in Detroit than in Toledo, largely through the sheikh's assumption of a role of leadership not common in Sunni Islam. The office of the religious leader among Sunnis has no special authority or divine prestige. It is an instructive job which is acquired by secular means and the prestige of the religious leader comes from his personal qualifications and social station. The religious leader of the Shi'ahs, however, is invested with a kind of divine authority. The rank of that divine authority varies in the different Shi'ah sects from complete divine authority, as among Ismailis, to the moderate form accepted in the Detroit community. In fact, the educated Shi'ahs in Detroit understand the historical-political origins of Shi'aism and look upon it as a genealogical identification rather than a distinct religious identification, distinguishing themselves from the Sunnis. They work openly to undermine the authority of the Shi'ah sheikh in their midst.

CHAPTER FOUR

Generation

In the vast sociological literature of social change among immigrant groups that assimilate a new culture and leave traditions behind, there is a special emphasis on generations. The first-generation immigrant is the carrier of a different culture which is transmitted to the new generation. This new generation is born in a different culture from that of the first-generation immigrants. The amalgamation of the different cultural elements of the old and new often creates two kinds of conflict: psychological and social. The psychological conflict in the immigrant personality is much stronger in the second generation than in the first and third generations. The second-generation member is torn by direct pressures exerted on him by home and ethnic community, on the one hand, and by school and the larger society on the other. In his struggle to maintain the balance between the two cultural forces, the second-generation member develops a "marginal personality." This marginality between the two cultures is associated with the social conflict among the ethnic generations. The second generation, in its attempt to keep the cultural balance, often clashes with the first generation. The degree of that clash varies according to the degree of assimilation the first generation has achieved. The more assimilated to the new culture the first generation is, the less it clashes with the second generation. This situation helps to maintain the solidarity of the ethnic community around some other distinct criterion, like religion, if it is not in conflict with the new culture. But when the first generation is less assimilated, the clash with the second generation may result either in maladjustment or social deviation, both of which can reduce the ethnic community's moral and religious integration.

The degree of conflict between the second and third ethnic generations also very much depends on how much assimilation the first generation has achieved, for the second generation may be more repressive toward the third than the first generation toward the second. Thus the generation variable in the ethnic community is intercorrelated with the other social variables and can be studied in the light of the over-all position of the ethnic community in the larger society.

Generation in the Two Communities

The generation distribution in the Toledo and Detroit communities is shown in Table 35. Due to the relatively recent arrival of the Arab Moslems in the United States, the percentage of the first generation in general, and in Toledo in particular, is much larger than the third, in the ratio of 2 to 1 in the total sample and 3 to 1 in Toledo. As said before, the immigration of the Arab Moslems to the United States started at the turn of the twentieth century. This group had been attracted to South America about fifty years earlier. Their relatively late arrival on the American continents may mark the rediscovery period. The Arab Moslems proudly mention that their ancestors crossed the Atlantic from Spain and arrived at Brazil in the year 1150 A.D.[1] Before that, in the tenth century A.D., according to the Arab geographer al-Sharif al-Idrisi,[2] eight adventurous Arabs had sailed from Lisbon, Portugal trying to discover what lay beyond the sea of darkness, as the Arabs called the Atlantic. It is said that they landed at South America. Historians, however, deny that this story reported by al-Idrisi is assumed to have inspired Columbus to try to reach the East through the West, which led to the great discovery of America. In 1955, when Italy celebrated the five hundredth anniversary of the birth of Columbus, there was a fair at which many of Columbus' belongings were dis-

Table 35

Generation in Both Communities

Generation	*Toledo*		*Detroit*		*Total*	
	No.	%	No.	%	No.	%
First	86	41	60	28	146	35
Second	97	46	102	48	199	47
Third	28	13	49	24	77	18
Total	211	100	211	100	422	100

[1] Yacub Audat, *al-Natiqun bildād fi Amerika al-Ganubiyya* (Beirut, 1956), pp. 5-17.

[2] *Ibid.*

played. Included was an Arabic book, said to be the Idrisi book, in which the author mentioned the story of the eight adventurers. It is not the purpose here to verify such claims. It suffices to point to the fact that migration is one characteristic of the Arabs because of their nomadic history. But if the early migration was initiated by personal curiosity, the late one was initiated by social causes.

Causes of Migration

Arab Moslem migration to the United States resulted from the two causes Warner and Srole give for migration of other ethnic groups: "forces of attraction exerted by the expanding American economy and forces of expulsion exerted in the lands of emigration."[3]

In response to the question "Why did you leave your country?" 45.9 per cent of the first-generation immigrants cited economic reasons, while 45.2 per cent said that it was because either one or more members of their families were in America, or that the husband or wife had been in America before, as Table 36 shows.

Their source of information about the United States was mainly through either relatives or friends who had migrated before them. In response to the question "How did you know about the United States?" (Table 37), 80.2 per cent of the first-generation immigrants mentioned relatives, while 14.4 per cent mentioned reputation through friends.

TABLE 36

Distribution of the First-Generation Respondents by Reasons for Leaving the Native Country

	No.	%
1. Economic conditions	67	45.9
2. One or more members of the family in America	38	26
3. Spouse was in America	28	19.2
4. Personal ambition	5	3.4
5. Political reasons	3	2
6. Education	1	0.7
7. No reason	4	2.8
Total	146	100.0

[3] Lloyd W. Warner and Leo Srole, *The Social System of American Ethnic Groups* (New Haven, 1945), p. 105.

TABLE 37
How First-Generation Respondents Knew about America before Their Migration

	No.	%
1. Through relatives already in the United States	65	44.5
2. Spouse had been in the U. S.	30	20.6
3. Parent was a U. S. Citizen	22	15.1
4. Reputation through friends	21	14.4
5. Through friends in the U. S.	2	1.4
6. Movies	3	2.0
7. Reading	3	2.0
Total	146	100.0

The short visits of the pioneers, displaying their superiority in the home country, inspired youth to follow the same path to wealth and adventure. Hence, the majority of the first generation —61 per cent—came to America as unmarried young men (Table 38). Of the married immigrants, 86.2 per cent came either alone or with just the spouse; only 12.1 per cent came with the whole family, including spouse and children.

The attraction of the United States was greatest among the lower socio-economic class. The hard economic conditions which drove the emigrants from the old countries impelled them also to seek economic success at any cost. Most of the first-generation immigrants admitted that they did not intend to establish themselves permanently in the United States. They just hoped to collect the most money in the shortest possible time and then go back, buy a piece of land, get married, and live a happy, wealthy life among their kinfolk. America was, to the early immigrant, a land of dreams, where abundance was available for all. When the immigrant lands and faces social and economic difficulties he never dreamed of, he is greatly disappointed. Nevertheless, he is willing to bear the hardship and struggles to overcome these difficulties for many reasons. Once he decides to leave his original country he assumes an heroic role in his extended family and community. He is looked upon as the economic savior of his nuclear family. He is the social star, at least in his own image, in the eyes of the girls of his community. He is going to America, the dream of everyone. Sustained by these images of himself, he does not surrender very easily to failure in America.

TABLE 38

Marital Status of the First-Generation Respondents at the Time They Emigrated

Married and Came to America:	No.	%
Alone	9	15.5
Before spouse	3	5.2
After spouse	13	22.4
With spouse only	25	43.1
With children only	1	1.7
With whole family wife and children	7	12.1
Total	58	100.0

Single and Came to America:	No.	%
Alone	45	50.6
With friends	15	16.9
With relatives (other than parents)	13	14.6
With one parent only	6	6.7
With parents only	1	1.1
With whole family (parents and siblings)	8	10.1
Total	88	100.0

Many first-generation respondents told the investigator about hundreds of dollars they had sent home while they were struggling along in the early period in America. They did this not merely as a gesture of charity toward poor relatives but also—perhaps primarily—to acquire prestige and maintain the aura of importance they had enjoyed when they left. They do not write home about the difficulties, but exaggerate what they own. An immigrant living in a furnished room may tell his friends and relatives back home that he owns a villa. If he buys a 1960 Ford he may write that he bought a 1966 Cadillac. Apparently these reports of affluence help to stir the envy of the other youth. Moslem applicants for entry to the United States continue to exceed the yearly quota. The first immigrants themselves probably have been the victims of such reports about the new magic world in the local newspapers and from the reputation acquired through the stories of those who had pioneered.

Language

Responding to the question "What did you find most difficult when you first came to America?" 97 per cent of the first-generation respondents reported that learning the English language was the most difficult adjustment to make. Coming from the lower educational class and having acquired no knowledge of English before their emigration, they found everything very strange to them in America. The majority of the first generation of Toledo and Detroit had to cluster around some pioneers in order to solve the critical linguistic problem. This linguistic handicap probably has been one of the most influential factors in erecting the ghettos and ethnic residential sections in the Moslems' American urban life. The less English-speaking an ethnic community in America, the more clannish it is and the more it segregates itself from American life. That segregation delays the process of assimilation.

But with time and new generations, the ethnic groups manage to solve the language problem and thus to become gradually absorbed into their new culture. For our sample, 83 per cent in Toledo now speak and read English, against 76 per cent in Detroit (Table 39). This difference between the two communities, in favor of Toledo, occurs despite the fact that there is a higher proportion of first-generation members in Toledo than in Detroit.

TABLE 39

Distribution of First-Generation Respondents on Speaking and Reading English, in Both Communities

	Toledo		*Detroit*	
	No.	%	No.	%
Do not speak or read	15	7	19	9
Speak only	21	10	32	15
Speak and read	175	83	160	76
Totals	211	100	211	100

The literature on ethnic groups shows that the correlation between generation and this linguistic factor is very strong, and this is borne out in our sample, as Table 40 shows. This linguistic factor may cause conflict within the Arabs' family life in America. The open American social structure motivates the second generation of these two communities to climb higher in socioeconomic status, but the relatively higher internalization of the American values in Toledo's first generation reduces this tendency to family conflict. In the two communities together, 21 per cent of the first generation do not speak English while 20 per cent of the second generation and 71 per cent of the third do not speak Arabic, as shown in Table 41.

It is possible that the 20 per cent of the non-Arabic-speaking second generation understand the everyday words they hear at home. They most likely understand their mother tongue to a certain degree, but they cannot answer in Arabic. When the parent in such a family does not speak English (as is often the case), the communication between the first and second generation is reduced to a minimum, though the lack of communication is sharper between the first and third generations.

TABLE 40

Generation on Speaking and Reading English

	First		*Second*		*Third*	
	No.	%	No.	%	No.	%
Do not speak or read	31	21	2	1	0	0
Speak only	47	32	8	4	1	1
Speak and read	68	47	189	95	76	99
Totals	146	100	199	100	77	100

TABLE 41

Generations on Speaking and Reading Arabic

	First		*Second*		*Third*	
	No.	%	No.	%	No.	%
Do not speak or read	0	0	40	20	55	71
Speak only	55	38	119	60	21	27
Speak and read	91	62	40	20	1	2
Totals	146	100	199	100	77	100

Despite the fact that the first-generation pities the third-generation member who is, in the former's eyes, "lost," the behavior of the first-generation seems to be more sympathetic toward the third than toward the second-generation. The third-generation also pities the first-generation member for his "backwardness."

If the different behavior and outlook on life between the first and third generations are attributed to differences in time and thus taken for granted, the different behavior and outlook of the second generation are considered deviations by the first generation. There is no visible struggle between the first and third generations because of conditions each generation recognizes as insurmountable. The struggle exists between the first generation, still socially active, and the second generation, exposed to different values. It is a conflict between equally irreconcilable powers. One is equipped with deep traditions and the other is armed with more freedom of action. The conflict between generations has several roots and manifests itself in various social forms.

ROOTS OF CONFLICT BETWEEN GENERATIONS

Education

Most of the first-generation immigrants have had little or no formal education. The family in the old country performed many functions which, in the more complex societies, are performed by specialized separate institutions. Although the school was the formal educational institution, difficult economic conditions prevented that institution from serving as large a group as in the more economically advanced countries. The agrarian family needed the complete participation of all its members. The children simply could not be spared for formal education. Thus the main education a child could obtain was in the tradition transmitted from one generation to another. The parents were the vocational trainers and educators.

Since the emphasis in knowledge and wisdom was on the past, parents achieved status in the family through experiences which were associated with old age. The traditional admiration for the aged in less literate societies derives from that association between experience and old age, as accentuated in folklore. In more literate, industrialized societies, the emphasis in knowledge is on science and technology. Knowledge is not tied to the past. The machine and space era, with its emphasis on scientific achievement for the future, has shifted family status from the aged to the young. The function of traditional education in the home, to solidify the family under the control of the aged, has given way to a new concept of education.

The tradition-oriented first-generation Moslem in America is puzzled by the independence and even the disobedience of his children. He often expresses his disappointment about the new pattern of family relations by saying "We lost our children in America," for they still dream of the patriarchal pattern which they imagine, incorrectly, to be unchanged in the old country. But the attitudes of the first generation puzzle the second generation too. As Warner puts it,

> Not only does the child resent the fact that his parents do not act after the American behavioral norms; not only does he resent pressure to act after the ethnic behavioral modes; but, infused with American social logics, he implicitly questions the right of his father to dominate and control his behavior.[4]

The demand for freedom by the second generation conflicts with the desire of the first to retain control. This is the cornerstone of generational conflict. The more traditional the first-generation members, the more they demand control over the second generation and the wider the differences become, as indeed they have in the Detroit community.

The Detroit Moslem of the second generation is born into two different cultures and grows up under both influences. In time the influence of his family is outweighed by the influence of the American culture. Once he goes out to play with American children he encounters the fear and fascination of a new language.

[4] W. Lloyd Warner, *Structure of American Life* (Edinburgh, 1952), p. 125.

By the time he goes to school his English vocabulary is the dominant one. The different symbols of the American language (especially slang concerning dates, girl friends and boy friends) convey to him lighter, easier values which differ from the more ponderous values of his family. As Warner observes, "Here the schools function to orient the children to the new American society and away from their traditional group."[5]

Communication among generations in the family is manifested in the language both generations use at home. Linguistically, the family pattern has become heterogeneous; the first generation speaks in Arabic, but the second generation answers in English. Not only is English easier for the second-generation member: it is superior. He sees the struggles of his parents to express themselves in English and their use of English words in Arabic constructions. Though the children laugh at their efforts, parents learn a great deal of English from their children—and a great deal, as well, about the American way of life. The crucial point comes, as Warner says, when "the child, not the parent, becomes the transmitting agent of social change."[6]

Education is therefore a major reason why the younger generation of both communities have become the agent of social change. This sharp educational difference among generations, especially between the first and second, is one of the factors responsible for family conflict in these two ethnic communities. The family has become less integrated as each generation has come to look at the other from its own position and values.

Also associated with the family conflict is the first generation's strong resistance to the social change introduced by the younger generation. Since the new environment continuously strengthens the value standards of the younger American-born generation over those of the first immigrant generation, the latter group is always frustrated in what is for them a losing battle. The Toledo first-generation members have been wise enough to surrender community leadership to the members of the second generation; the Detroit first-generation members still struggle to maintain domination. The different attitudes of the first toward the second generation in these two communities reflect the different patterns of family relation.

Being even more tradition-bound than the people now in the

[5] *Ibid.*, p. 124.
[6] *Ibid.*, p. 126.

old country, the Moslem of the Detroit first generation still seeks to retain the old pattern of authoritarian control in his family as well as his community relations. Ghetto-like Dearborn has barred the first generation from realizing the change in time and place. The authoritarian father is developed in an agrarian culture. In the farming communities, the father is the patriarch and the center of social and economic activities. He is also the law-giver and he controls the family's behavior, money, and division of labor.

The father in the Detroit community finds his traditional authority challenged by his children who are exposed to the new culture through the educational media. The resistance of the first generation is met by stronger resistance from the second generation and these unbalanced opposite forces between generations in the family relations have resulted in the father's failure to maintain the traditional style. "He does not know how to control the children," is the common complaint of the Detroit wife against her husband. "The children," she continues, "don't listen to us. They spend most of their time out. They just come home to eat and sleep."

What the new Detroit generation members complain about is the failure of traditional family structure to hold their loyalty. Nothing in the unpleasant home atmosphere attracts them. The disintegration of the family structure manifests itself in numerous patterns, ranging from conversation to food. The parents' conversation is centered around persons and families, taking the concrete shape of gossip. The children's conversation is centered around cars, nights, pleasures outside the home, and even general social problems. The parents still love the Syrian dishes which the children do not appreciate at all. Very often, the housewife cooks *mijaddara* or *Kebba nayya* for herself and her husband and something else for her children. A second-generation member of the Detroit community summed up in three words the view of his generation toward their parents: "They neglect life," he said. Asked to elaborate, he replied:

> I don't remember that my parents ever took us out to dinner, movies, or theater. They never invited any American family or accepted any American invitation. The reason is that my mother does not speak English. When I bought my car, they were angry at me. I don't have complete freedom to spend my money. I work for my father. He gives me much less than what I could get working outside. Despite this they watch what I spend as if I were

spending their money. Next year I'll be thirty years old but they still deal with me as if I were a child. If I buy a new suit or spend my vacation in Florida with some American friends they cry that I'm spoiled, that I spend too much on my friends, and so on. I'm sick of this life.

The "Beat" Arab Generation in Detroit

The first generation, exerting on their children the pressures of traditional habits and attitudes, impose severe social strain on the second generation. This younger generation is forced to attempt a reconciliation between the two distinct cultures; this accounts for their social and religious break with the first generation. Their forms of deviation represent the psychological outlets of the suppressed second-generation personality.

Detroit is said to owe much of its night life activities to the Moslem "beat" generation. Barred by the authoritarian first generation from an active role in the Moslem community, most of the young generation members have swung radically from the mores of both cultures, indulging in night life to satisfy their unsublimated desires. Even within the community demarcation in Dearborn, Dix Street manifests the sharp deviation of the young generation. Scores of idle, jobless young men form several cliques which cluster here and there on the street corners, in billiard rooms, and in the coffeehouses where gambling is very common. Their loud conversations are meaningless and often end in fighting.

Such behavior results from idleness in the industrial society. The recent economic recession which hit Detroit heavily added considerable weight to the already alarming social problem of unemployment. Having no seniority in their work, most of the members of the Detroit young generation were laid off and have been since then, with neither work nor income to meet the increasing economic demands caused by constant out-of-work activities. This situation made the members of the Detroit's young Moslem generation feel antagonistic toward life in America. The new affection for the old countries which they have developed may be attributed to their discontent about the present economic conditions in America as well as to their hope of getting technical positions in the prosperous Arab countries. Responding to the question "What, in general, have you found least satisfying about life in America?", a score of the young generation answered, "Nothing to do, staying in one place, and lack of money."

As we have implied, this behavior of Detroit's young generation is also the result of cultural discontinuity. The traditionalistic, authoritarian attitudes of the first generation have had two adverse effects on the young. On the one hand, the old, unmodified cultural values could not be accepted by the American-educated young generation. Thus the old culture has ceased to be transmitted through the rigid first generation. On the other hand, the new American cultural values carried by the young generation are resisted by the first; the new culture is no longer transmitted to the community through the ethnic medium of the second generation. Instead of positive cultivation of the two cultures to achieve a sufficient degree of equilibrium, the uncooperative attitudes of both generations have resulted in mutual evasion of each other's values. Thus the cultural values of each have remained within each and alien to the other.

The twofold effect of the first generation's attitudes is very obvious in the sphere of religion. This generation's traditionalistic approach to religion has weakened religious practices in the community. The mosque is still seen by the Detroit members as a place for men. Even in the rear ranks they do not tolerate participation by women. As a result, the youth associate the mosque with the aged and the backward. Those who attend Friday prayer do not exceed 6 per cent of the old-generation males; this low percentage is, again, the result of retaining the old traditions. The Shi'ahs' instructions do not oblige them to pray in the mosque on Fridays. In their eyes, the mosque is a Sunni institution and, retaining the traditional sectarian dispute, no single Shi'ah member attends Friday prayer in the mosque. In addition, it often happens that the Sunni imam is busy with his secular or religious activities outside Detroit and thus Friday prayer is necessarily suspended.

Toledo Family Pattern

The Toledo community provides a contrast to Detroit, where the rigidity of tradition has enlarged the gulf between the generations. The moderate liberal attitudes of this community's first generation toward the second have minimized potential conflict and enabled religious activities to flourish. The Toledo community represents a pattern of selectivity: its members, due to their long period of exposure to the American culture before establishing the community, had internalized to a high degree the American values, and they planned Toledo as an American-Moslem community.

The members did not come directly from the old country to gather haphazardly in one area where the traditional values are preserved: they migrated to the community from other American states where they had lived among Americans. The occupational pattern of liquor is strong evidence of such Americanization. The purpose of establishing the community was to preserve the Islamic religious identification in support of their social status as American middle class. That social-religious decision was taken after realizing the psychological commitment of establishing their life permanently in America.

Thus the intention to settle permanently in America was made early by the Toledo first generation because of their economic success. This decision helped them to adjust to the new environment. The deceptive attitude of, "when we go back to the old country, our children will learn a lot about their religion" did not emerge among them. The Toledo first-generation members realized their new minority status in the new environment. Having committed themselves to a permanent settlement, they accepted and welcomed the inevitable associate factor of being American. But being American, they saw, does not mean being without religion; rather, good Americans are in favor of religious affiliation. The first-generation members conveyed to the second the common ethical values of America and the old country in terms of religion and they accepted from the second generation the new American norms, mores, and social habits. This reciprocity between the two generations permitted the joining of the two cultural streams and resulted in an integral American Moslem community. The traditionalistic sectarian values which separated Sunnis from Shi'ahs in the old country disappeared, at least from public view.

Many secular elements have penetrated religion in the Toledo community. On Sunday, when the first- and second-generation parents bring their children to Sunday school at the mosque, most of them pray without ablution. This habit is not institutionalized, however, for the parents do not proclaim it as a principle that ablution must be avoided; they explain the practice this way:

> Ablution was introduced to the nomadic communities in the absence of hygienic habits and instructions. But now, under the sanitary conditions of our day in this country, everyone is supposed to be clean—thus ablution has lost its function as a precondition for prayer.

Also, among the second generation in both communities, 82 per cent do not even know that a bath is religiously required after sexual intercourse. Rationalizations of these changes encourage the congregation to participate fully in the religious practices without hidden restrictions. This kind of secularization conforms to the American religious patterns in which tradition often gives way to rationalization.

Leadership in the Toledo community's social activities as well as the religious teachings is held mainly by the American-oriented, second-generation females. In their relations with the other religious groups as well as teaching their younger generation, they stress the social and religious ethics and religious tolerance of Islam. "To be a good Moslem you have to be a good American and vice versa," this writer heard a young woman tell her Sunday school class. "Islam acknowledges and respects the other heavenly religions. It came to abolish human inequality on the basis of language, nation or race. It preaches human brotherhood."

This religious moderation and orientation of the Toledo second generation has kept Islamic self-identification compatible with Americanism. The social changes in the family and community relations between the Toledo first and second generations have taken the American direction, where the older generation plays a guiding, but not a leading, role. The Toledo first-generation parents adjusted themselves to the more American role of providing affection in a conjugal family rather than of acting as the authority. This adjustment in the family has made it possible to build community solidarity with a minimum of revolt or deviation by the younger generation.

Generation and Religious Consciousness

One of the major difficulties in measuring attitudes and values among the three generations is that they differ in their degrees of awareness of what is happening to them. The first generation is more conscious of old ideals and values than the second and third generations. The discrepancy between ideals and facts, between what the tradition commands and what is actually done, diminishes the value of certain questionnaire data; to minimize the shortcoming of the statistical analyses, therefore, the data must be supplemented by direct observation.

To check on the accuracy of generation responses, we asked parents some questions about the religious practices of their children. The first generation does not understand the second generation as well as the second generation understands the third. Comparing the parents' answers with those of their children, we found that 53 per cent of the first-generation parents and 27 per cent of the second-generation parents exaggerate the religious fidelity of their children. Furthermore, the writer noticed that the majority of the first-generation members tend to practice their religion and accurately report facts about their adherence to religious tradition, whereas the majority of the second generation do not practice but report that they do practice. During Ramadan, the month of fasting, many second-generation members falsely claimed to be fasting. In the coffeehouses, some of them drank tea and coffee during the day while they claimed to be fasting.

The adherence to the formal conventions of religion is not so strong in the third generation as in the second. The majority of the third generation do not practice their religion, but they do not hide this fact. They often rationalize it.

Religious orientation is not significantly associated with attitudes toward Arab nationalism. The third generation, which is less religiously conscious than the second, is more politically oriented toward Arab nationalism. *Its political orientation is similar to that of the first generation.*

Many factors can be adduced to explain this political regression. The third-generation members cannot hide the fact that they are the descendants of Arabs. The recent political events in the Arab countries which accentuated the international focus on the Middle East for the present decade have been considerably discussed in the United States. The American-educated third generation has grown up during a period when American public opinion has been concerned with the Middle East. The recently unfavorable propaganda against the Arab countries throughout the American media has also aroused the sympathetic feeling of the third generation toward the countries of their ancestry.

This sympathetic Arab nationalism is much stronger in the third generation of Detroit than in that of Toledo. This is natural since it is a reaction to nationalistic propaganda, which is much stronger in Detroit than in Toledo.

On the other hand, the Toledo third generation is more religious than the Detroit third generation. This means that fidelity to tradition takes religious shape in Toledo and political shape in Detroit. The high degree of assimilation of the Toledo community weakens the Arab-nationalistic orientation of the community's third generation. In general, the higher the degree of assimilation in both communities, the lower the political orientation to Arab nationalism.

The relatively lower economic status of the Detroit community is another factor promoting the political orientation toward Arab nationalism. The economically secure and socially contented Toledo community feels no need to espouse Arab nationalism. Their nationalistic activities are motivated by the desire to promote their religious institutions. Whenever the community invites any prominent Arab personality, its purpose is to seek religious promotion by asking for religious teachers and support, or other religious encouragement from the Arab countries. This religious goal raises the community's prestige in the larger society. Nationalism is employed only as a means to that goal.

The Detroit third generation, on the other hand, is developing a special form of Arab nationalism. Economically, it is not well off: the recession of 1957 plus the increasing automation and decentralization of the auto industry have caused serious deterioration in the socio-economic condition of the new generation. The American-educated third generation dreams of making a new life in the countries of their ancestors. Many have expressed the desire to work there as technicians in the new boom of industrialization.

Arab nationalism is also stronger in Detroit because competition for community leadership between the two religious sects has weakened the emphasis on religion for its own sake. In contrast with Toledo, Detroit's religious activities are influenced by each sect's desire to appear more nationalistic than the other, in the expectation that this political sanction will lead to popularity and leadership. Thus, religion in Detroit, deriving its power from the Arab nationalism centered in Cairo, has become a means to social leadership.

The presidency of the Islamic Federation, shifted to Detroit in July 1959, has raised the political as well as social prestige of the community in the Arab countries, especially in the United Arab Republic. Doubtless the association between Arab nationalism and Islamic movements in Detroit is going to strengthen the community's political, social, and economic relations with the U.A.R. as the popular sponsor of both movements.

The social conflict between the first and third generation in Toledo is minimized by a kind of mutual compromise in which each generation tolerates the social attitudes of the other. The first generation's compromise is reflected in their higher degree of assimilation, while the third generation compromise by achieving a relatively high degree of religiosity. Thus each generation exhibits an awareness of, and a respect for, the attitudes of the other. The relatively low degree of both assimilation and religiosity in the two Detroit generations is evidence of the opposite situation, i.e., the sharp conflict in that community between the first and third generations. Another positive factor in Toledo is the mediatory role held by the second generation; this has helped to minimize the conflict, while the negative role of the Detroit second generation may be responsible in part for the sharp conflict between the two generations.

Generation and Occupation

Occupational data by generations reveal interesting similarities and differences. In Toledo, the majority of the second and third generations tend to follow the business pattern of the first generation. Even professionals of these two generations invest their money and leisure time in the liquor business, as owners, or by helping their parents or relatives.

The Detroit second generation has deviated from the first in many ways. These younger people like neither factory work nor the grocery business—the principal occupations of the first generation. The second-generation members are either civil servants or professionals, or electric appliance businessmen. Table 42 shows the percentage distribution of the changing occupational pattern in Detroit in contrast with that of Toledo. The occupational shift of the Detroit second generation signals the disintegration of the family in the community.[7] The members of each family with their different occupations cannot even find a

[7] Daniel R. Miller and Guy E. Swanson, *The Changing American Parent: A Study in the Detroit Area* (New York, 1958), p. 236.

TABLE 42

Occupational Patterns of the First and Second Generations in Both Communities in Per Cent

*Occupation**	*Toledo*		*Detroit*	
	1st	2nd	1st	2nd
Civil service	0	3	2	19
Professional	2	14	1	18
Electric appliance business	0	0	0	16
Factory work (unskilled)	13	11	39	15
Bar, restaurant ownership	56	55	3	2
Grocery business	3	4	14	2
Other	12	11	6	13
Retired	14	0	24	0
Unemployed	0	2	11	15
Totals	100	100	100	100

* These occupational categories are not in conformity with any sociological conventional categories. They just show the prevailing patterns in both communities.

common theme of interest to guide their conversation. In fact, they scarcely find a chance to talk to one another or exchange thoughts. Except for the second-generation husband, every unmarried working member comes home at irregular times to swallow his dinner hastily and then run out to join his friends. The mother very often serves daily as many dinners as there are adult children. There is, moreover, little sympathy even among brothers and sisters.

In Toledo, the homogeneous occupational pattern of the first and second generations is a sign of relative stability in the general community, as well as in the family structure, against the rapidly and continuously changing social conditions. There are mutual themes of interest on which the family members focus their attention. The religious and social activities of the second generation please the first generation.

As has been seen, the social relations between the second and third generations differ between the two communities. The marginality of Detroit's second generation has diverted the third generation from Moslem community life, while the assimilation of the second generation in Toledo has allowed the third generation to be absorbed into the Moslem community.

However, the third generation in both communities has reached a high degree of assimilation. This degree is perhaps the ceiling which is reached by the typical young American generation. No centrifugal force that is much stronger than the mere absence of attraction in the community need be exerted on the ethnic third generation. The absorptive forces in the American open-class structure are unique. In the absence of highly distinctive physical traits and color, the American open-class system operates to disturb the two Moslem communities by allowing their members to move quickly, according to their merits and achievements. The ethnic children respond to the attraction of the class system by breaking their ethnic ties and identifying with the social symbols of the new culture. Unless the second generation is able to come closer to the degree of assimilation of the third generation, the community ties between the two generations tend to break, as they have in Detroit.

Contrary to an implication in Warner,[8] the persistence of group identification is not necessarily associated with resistance to assimilation. The strong religious identification of the Toledo community does not hinder the process of assimilation; rather, it accelerates it. Furthermore, though they differ significantly in religious identification, the third generations in both communities have achieved a similar high degree of assimilation. The Toledo third generation (although proportionally smaller than its peer in Detroit) has added to the Moslem community by maintaining good relations with the second generation, whereas in Detroit the third generation has not really become a part of a Moslem community. There is an absence of reciprocity between traditions and modernization.

[8] Warner, *op. cit.*, p. 118.

CHAPTER FIVE

Religiosity

The religion of the Toledo and Detroit communities will be treated here as a factor seen in two distinct analytical ways. In one case, religion will be treated as a dependent variable: an effect of numerous other institutional factors. In the second, it will be viewed as an independent variable, or a "mover" of other institutional factors.

The first approach leads to the examination of religion within the frame of its social surroundings; these include (1) the influence of the time factor in an alien culture; (2) the ecological factor of concentrating or scattering the members of the community in the larger society; (3) the exposure to or participation in the broader way of life, in contrast to remaining in the ghetto of old customs and traditions that may not fit the new environment; (4) the type of generation holding the social leadership in both communities; and (5) the existence or absence of religious leaders. The second approach leads to the discussion of how these factors and other institutions seem to have been influenced by the Islamic religion. In summary, the religion of these two communities will be considered in light of the general theoretical problems of assimilation and adaptation of immigrant groups to their new culture.

All religious measurements developed for this study are derived from the Islamic instructions. It must be recognized, therefore, that no attempt is made here to measure the extent to which the American Moslem communities are more or less religious, according to these jurisprudential criteria, than contemporary communities in Lebanon, Egypt and Pakistan, for example, or than historical Moslem communities of previous generations. The sole purpose here is to make some estimate of the extent to which the respondents in the American Moslem communities have deviated from the religious practices in which they engaged while still in "the old country." The jurisprudential criteria of religious observance are therefore used here simply as guidelines for measurement of the differences between current practices of the sample of respondents and their former practices, and thus to get some estimate of the impact of American life upon their religious practices. Similarly, when we compare the religious practices of the different generations of Moslems in our American samples, the conclusions about change will be relative to generational differences alone, without any intention to compare, even implicitly, the American Moslems with "old country" counterparts.

Religious and Cultural Backgrounds of the Two Communities

The two communities have identical religio-ethnic backgrounds to the extent that both are exclusively Moslem and predominantly Lebanese, with a few families from Syria and Palestine. However, the majority of the members like to be referred to as Syrians, for most of the first-generation immigrants left the old country while it bore that name. After Syria gained political independence in 1948, which made Lebanon a distinctive political entity on a religious basis, the immigrants who had come to America from what is now called Lebanon felt less associated with that almost half Christian country and more oriented toward the historical unity of the two sections called Syria. Their sentimental orientation, therefore, is toward that historical entity and not toward the distinctive political section, Syria. However, the absolute unity among the Arab states within a federal system or a complete political mergence into one big nation directed from any Arab country is the dream of the great majority of Arabs; as positively expressed in our sample, 78 per cent are in favor of such a mergence, against 9 per cent opposed, and 13 per cent unconcerned or in doubt.

The Present Religious Situations of the Two Communities

But though Toledo and Detroit Moslems share this background identification, it was found that they differ significantly in their degree of religiosity. Furthermore, the difference is not only one of degree: each community practices a different *kind* of religion. Surprisingly enough, the religious patterns of the two communities are not compatible with the prevailing laws of assimilation which indicate that the more the ethnic group loses in its traditions, the more assimilated it is to the new culture. How all these factors can be accounted for is the main concern of this chapter.

The Measurement of Religiosity

Briefly, it was possible to construct a scale of religiosity such that respondents could be classified into high, middle, low and deviant, the last referring to those respondents whose religious practices and senses of affiliation are either too attenuated and/or too vague to permit them to be classified as members of any religious group or in any way religiously observant. The distribution of these four religious classes by the two communities is shown in Table 43. When the total sample is dichotomized into just a high and low group, with the latter containing the low and the deviant groups, it is found that 60 per cent of the Toledo group scores high as against 36 per cent of the Detroit group.

Traditionally speaking, Islam has been a male religion; that is, the women are not encouraged to participate in the socially religious activities, such as praying at the mosque and performing pilgrimage. If a woman cannot find a close relative to accompany her, she is not required to perform pilgrimage. Indeed, if she performs it alone, her pilgrimage is religiously questionable. Friday noon prayer in Islam must be performed at the mosque in a group; this religious observance is waived for the women. In fact, Omar, the second caliph, observing the looseness of sexual morality caused by new wealth, which created a leisure class, asked women to pray at home instead of attending congregational prayers at the mosque. He could not totally restrict the freedom of women to attend the mosques, but he greatly preferred to see them pray at home and took measures for persuading them to do so. In this respect, Islamic traditions are very much like Hebraic

TABLE 43

The Four Classes of Religiosity-Scale by the Two Communities

Community	*High*		*Middle*		*Low*		*Deviant*	
	No.	%	No.	%	No.	%	No.	%
Toledo	64	60	63	65	52	42	32	33
Detroit	43	40	33	35	71	58	64	67
Total	107	100	96	100	123	100	96	100

traditions, in which the congregation is considered primarily a community for males.

Christianity differs in this respect from both Islam and Judaism. The Christian church is the place for both sexes; indeed, Christian women have become even more socially religious than men. This Western religious influence can be seen very clearly in the Toledo community. The social religious role of the Toledo community is played so much by the women that the fine Toledo mosque may be attributed to the efforts of the women of the community.

These women participate in a variety of activities to support the mosque institution. One of their more popular fund-raising activities is selling tickets and serving dinners of Middle Eastern dishes in the basement of the mosque. Another activity is baking Middle Eastern pastries, which they sell for maintaining the mosque. They also arrange picnics during the summer for the families of the community, and they have joint activities with the Youth Club. Their branch, called the American Moslem Society Ladies Auxiliary, has 60 active members who meet frequently at the mosque to discuss social affairs. Many decisions of the main American Moslem Societies are delegated to this Ladies Auxiliary. The women are the sole teachers in Sunday school. Even in their religious lectures at the mosque and at other churches and social organizations, the women are very active and speak with authority and intelligence about Islam.

Had it not been for the activities of the women of Moslem communities, it may be truly said that the Moslem religious movement in America would not be as steady and strong as it is now. The social religious activities of these women is the product of the Western influence and of their assimilation in the new environment. The difference between the religious social activities of the Toledo and the Detroit communities is partly attributed to the different degrees of assimilation achieved by the women in both communities. More assimilated to the Western environment, the women in the Toledo community are more active in the mosque affairs than the women in the Detroit community who still hold the tradition that the mosque is the community of males. These women have not yet taken as full a share in the mosque affairs as have the women in the Toledo community.

This difference between the two communities is very significant at a level of .01. It is also found to be significant on every subscale. As the two communities differ in many social characteristics, despite their identical religio-ethnic background, this study is pursued in the light of "socio-cultural determinism." It is now desirable to examine this difference between the two communities in religiosity and relate it to its social association.

The Association between Sex and Religiosity

It was earlier hypothesized that the American Moslem females are generally more religious than males. This difference is said to result from the fact that the males communicate and mix more with the outside environment than females, who are more occupied with domestic activities. The male is more exposed to the host culture and the social process of acculturation than the female, and she retains the characteristics of the old culture. In our sample for both communities, this theory does not hold at all, for no significant difference could be observed between the sexes on the over-all scale of religiosity.

Occupation and Religiosity

The Toledo community differs from Detroit in patterns of occupation. The majority in Toledo have their own businesses, while most of the people in Detroit are blue-collar workers. It was expected that this difference would be associated with differences in religiosity: this proposition, however, was not found to be true in our sample. The difference between kinds of occupations on the scale of religiosity was not very significant.

Socio-Economic Status and Religiosity

In the literature of social stratification, the middle class has been found to be more religious than the higher or lower class. Controlling the other variables in our sample to examine the degree of association between the variables of socio-economic status and religiosity, we found their association to be weak and insignificant. The observed difference in religiosity between the two communities cannot, therefore, be accounted for by the difference in socio-economic status.

Education and Religiosity

It is true that religion is enhanced by a certain degree of education. To one who is educated, higher education tends to widen the area of humanity to include other people with other religions.

Education changes values and modifies attitudes. Before studying our sample, we hypothesized that there would be a negative correlation between education and religiosity. This hypothesis was examined and proved true. The difference among the three educational classes in the two communities taken together is found to be significant on the scale of religiosity. This finding is logical. If the community higher in religiosity is lower in educational achievement, and if the communities' differences in education prove to be significant, education may then be considered a decisive social variable to explain the differences in religiosity between the two communities.

Education by the Two Communities

Business ownership yields more profit than labor and employment; thus the hope for the laborer is to see his children on a higher occupational level. In open societies, where the main factor in occupying high professional jobs is acquired through free competition based on achievement, the most effective means to enhance one's status is education. Business needs empirical experience obtained through practice and does not necessarily require a high degree of education. Toledo, therefore, was thought to be educationally lower than Detroit. Educational differences were found between the two communities, but these were not significant. The difference in religiosity between the two communities thus cannot be accounted for by the educational difference.

Generation and Religiosity

It is maintained that there is a high positive correlation between generation and religiosity: the first generation, or the one closest to it, is higher on the scale of religiosity than the succeeding generations. This theory has its logic and supporting literature. The first-generation immigrants, brought up under the influence of a distinctly different culture, find that of the host country strange to them. Thus they begin to re-evaluate and cherish their old culture whose nucleus is religion. Religion is more strongly adhered to, at least in the area of belief and convention, by the first-generation immigrants than by those remaining in the old country. But as traditional values diminish in time, the second generation develops new attitudes toward both the old and new cultures. Religion, the last pride of man, tends to survive the crucial re-evaluative period. The third generation, more remote from the first than the second, is also further removed in tradition and religion.

Another theory, that of social regression, holds that the third generation tends to be more religious, though not more traditionalistic, than the second generation. Which path did these two communities actually take? In other words, is the third generation more or less religious than the second? A simple answer to this question is very misleading. There is, *in general*, a decline in religiosity from the first to the second to the third generation. This decline, as shown in Tables 44 and 45 is significant at a level of .01.

Tables 44 and 45 clearly support the first theory and show that the third generation is religiously more remote—from the first—than the second generation. As we observed earlier the negative correlation (although not significant) between education and religiosity, we may now establish this tentative proposition: the

TABLE 44

Scale of Religiosity by Generation

	CLASS OF RELIGIOSITY							
Generation	*High*		*Middle*		*Low*		*Deviant*	
	No.	%	No.	%	No.	%	No.	%
First	59	55	47	49	34	28	6	6
Second	36	34	43	45	66	54	54	56
Third	12	11	6	6	23	18	36	38
Totals	107	100	96	100	123	100	96	100

TABLE 45

Generation by Scale of Religiosity

	GENERATION					
Religiosity	*First*		*Second*		*Third*	
	No.	%	No.	%	No.	%
High	59	41	36	18	12	15
Middle	47	32	43	22	6	8
Low	34	23	66	33	23	30
Deviant	6	4	54	27	36	47
Totals	146	100	199	100	77	100

more educated one is, the less religious he will be. This premise should be considered at a low level, for the concern is with the immigrants only and there is, therefore, no attempt to generalize from the analysis at this stage. The proposition is based on the fact that the first-generation members have a low educational background. Those of the members or their offspring who achieved a relatively high level of education did so in America and thus are more exposed to the American culture.

The association between education and generation is high. The third generation is more educated than the second and the second more than the first. Can we find here the answer to our question? Earlier, we noticed the difference in religiosity between Toledo and Detroit communities; now we have established the association between religiosity and the multi-variable of education-generation. Can we relate this difference in religiosity to the difference between the generational composition of the two communities? In Toledo the proportion of the first generation to the third is much higher than in Detroit.

The difference between the two communities in generational composition is significant at a level of .01. The first generation has received less education in the host schools than have the second and third generations; correlatively, the first generation is less exposed to the adopted culture and much stronger in native tradition, especially religion. Furthermore, the proportion of the first generation to the third is much higher in Toledo than in Detroit. And, as expected, Toledo was found to be higher in religiosity than Detroit. Because of these four conditions, it would be justifiable to establish the correlation between religiosity and generation and by this finding sustain the first sociological theory (positive correlation between generation and religiosity) and refute the second (social regression).

Religiosity in the Scheme of Generation

The above conclusion is somewhat misleading. Although supported by statistics, it tells only half of the story; what it tells us is that there is a strong positive correlation between the rank of generation and the degree of religiosity. Among the immigrants, the first-generation members are more religious and more tradition-oriented than the second and the second are more than the third. This scheme contrasts with the sociological theory of regression, which indicates that the third-generation members tend to lean back approaching the curve of the first generation from which the second generation deviated. In our sample, the third generation is going in the same direction as the second, thus going further and further away from the first generation.

To examine the authenticity of this finding, the scale of religiosity was broken down to subscales. As one scale, each subscale was correlated separately with the three generations in each of the communities. Second, the individual items of the subscale were also correlated with the same three generations in each community. This double measurement was made specifically to enable us to probe beneath the misleading surface and locate the sources of differences in the generations' social associations. The over-all scale of religiosity is composed of four subscales: (1) scale of belief; (2) scale of convention; (3) scale of knowledge; and (4) scale of observances. The last one is made up of two subscales and two items; these two subscales are: (a) abstinence from eating pork; and (b) abstinence from drinking. The two items are: (i) praying; and (ii) fasting.

The Scale of Religious Belief

There are three classes on the scale of belief: high, middle, and low. For the present purposes the scale's classes were dichotomized high versus middle and low. To compare the three generations within the two communities, we compared the high in each community, as shown in Table 46.

The difference between the two communities in the second and third generations appears sharply. The percentage of those who scored high in Toledo's third generation is very close to that of Detroit's second generation. In both communities the same general trend is found. The third generation is less religious than the

TABLE 46

Those of Three Generations in Each Community Who Scored High on the Belief Scale

Community	Generation: First		Second		Third	
	No.	%	No.	%	No.	%
Toledo	79	92	69	71	15	54
Detroit	53	88	58	57	19	39

second and the second less than the first. Can we take this finding to support the earlier one and claim that generation is the only major decisive factor in religious belief? Since, in comparison with Detroit, Toledo has relatively more first-generation immigrants and fewer third, are we justified in saying that Toledo community is more religious than Detroit *because* it has more first-generation and fewer third-generation members than Detroit? Generation *is* a major factor but it is not the only decisive one. No simple factor can be the only decisive variable in explaining any community attribute or human behavior. The difference between the three generations in both communities is not significant even at a level of .05. However, it is indicative and inviting to look for its roots.

The communities' generational difference on the scale of belief may be illustrated further by breaking down the scale into its five items and comparing the frequencies of each item (Table 47). There are three prevailing patterns in the comparative percentage of these five items. The first is that within its three generations, Toledo is generally higher than Detroit (agreement on the first item in Toledo's first and third generations in both is 100). The

TABLE 47

Components of Religious-Belief Scale: Agreement of Generations in Each Community

Scale's Component	*Community*	GENERATION *First* No.	%	*Second* No.	%	*Third* No.	%
1. There is a God	T	86	100	97	100	28	100
	D	60	100	99	97	49	100
2. There is only one God	T	86	100	94	97	23	82
	D	59	98	98	96	40	82
3. Muhammad is our Prophet	T	86	100	89	92	18	64
	D	58	97	85	83	30	16
4. Quran is God's book	T	85	99	80	83	17	61
	D	57	95	73	72	22	45
5. There is a Judgment Day	T	79	92	78	79	22	78
	D	54	90	68	67	21	44

second pattern is that there is a general decline in religious beliefs from the first generation to the second and from the second to the third. The further a generation is from the first, the weaker it is in the traditional religious beliefs. For the third pattern, there is a decreasing movement of belief from the first to the fifth item. The only exception is Toledo's third generation on item five; agreement on this item even exceeds that for Item #3.

To rearrange the five items in descending order, according to the agreement on belief of Toledo's third generation, we find the following order:

1. There is a God	100%
2. There is only one God	82%
3. There is a Judgment Day	78%
4. Muhammad is our Prophet	64%
5. Quran is God's Book	61%

This is the pattern of the Toledo third generation's departure from the traditional beliefs still held by the three generations in Detroit and by Toledo's first and second generations. This order of belief represents a shift to American patterns. It may be taken, among many other points soon to be described, as an advanced point in the process of assimilating the religious pattern of America's middle class.

The three items highest on the belief order of the Toledo third generation are general religious items shared by the prevailing religions in America: Protestantism, Catholicism, and Judaism. Belief in the Judgment Day is also a cornerstone in the three religions of Islam, Christianity, and Orthodox Judaism. The oneness of God, a characteristic of Islam and Judaism, became an accepted doctrine by many Christian sects.

Though the three high items of belief of Toledo's third generation showed similarity to both Moslem and American patterns of religious beliefs, Toledo's youngest generation departed from the former and came closer to the latter on the general order and degree of the rest of the items. The specific Islamic items which distinguish Moslems in their beliefs (Items #4 and #5) are lower in order and weaker in degree than the other general items. However, Toledo's third generation still scored higher than Detroit's on these two items.

The relatively low rank order of these two items in the Toledo third generation may be responsible for raising the general standard of religiosity among the three generations and thus preserving religious belief in that generation on almost the same level as that of the Detroit second generation (57 per cent in Detroit's second generation and 54 per cent in Toledo's third). The justification of this paradox will come toward the end of this chapter. It suffices now to say that this point is associated with others to come. One of these is convention.

The Scale of Convention

Convention, unlike belief, is more social than personal. It is the common customary usage to which the community conforms. According to this conformity on customs, values are preserved or changed and attitudes are developed. One may personally violate a customary usage, but he is conscious and aware of his violation. In his general evaluation of other members of his community, he takes as his yardstick the customary values of his community even though he himself may not live up to them.

The scale of convention is made up of nine items after breaking down the scale into its component items and arranging them in traditional order of importance (Table 48). Convention is relative, changing with time and space. It is hypothesized that

TABLE 48

Positive Responses to Religious Conventions, by Generation in Both Communities, in Per Cent

Items of Convention	GENERATION					
	Toledo			*Detroit*		
	1st	2nd	3rd	1st	2nd	3rd
1. Pray	99	93	86	88	88	80
2. Pray five times daily	95	84	64	92	86	55
3. Pray at mosque Friday noon	95	84	64	80	66	39
4. Give alms	96	97	86	98	80	47
5. Fast on Ramadan	99	93	64	97	75	61
6. Perform pilgrimage	94	90	64	90	67	37
7. A good Moslem should not eat pork	84	79	82	93	80	73
8. Should not drink	80	79	79	97	72	67
9. Should not accept usury	60	47	50	77	55	57
Averages	89	83	71	90	74	57

there is a strong association between convention and belief. One who is stronger in belief is expected to be stronger in convention. In terms of our sample, the third generation in general is expected to be weaker than the second and the first. The Detroit third generation is expected to be weaker than its peer generation in Toledo. These hypotheses are found to be true, as Table 49 shows.

We observe that the three generations in Toledo are higher than their peers in Detroit. We also observe that there is a decline in observance of convention from the first to the second to the third generation in each community. It is noticed, third, that Detroit's youngest generation deviates very sharply from the second and is thus remote from the first. In Toledo, the decline is very moderate. Finally, the sharp contrast between the two communities is seen in the third generation. Toledo's third generation is even higher on the scale than Detroit's second generation, meaning that the second generation in Detroit conforms less to the religious customs than the third generation in Toledo. Table 48 shows the following:

1. These items of religious convention which have social features and explicit social functions similar to those highly respected in the host society, such as almsgiving, remain generally high. On the rank order, those items shift higher from the second to the third generations, and higher within Toledo's three generations than within Detroit's.

2. Items that feature dogma, such as pilgrimage, although they have implicit social functions, decline on the rank order from one generation to another; the decline is more visible in Toledo than in Detroit within peer generations.

3. As Toledo inclines toward general religious beliefs, it is also oriented toward general religious convention. Toledo is found to be higher than Detroit in general prayer. As it is a business community, Toledo is more moderate than Detroit on the usury item

TABLE 49

Positive Responses on the Convention Scale, by Generation, in Both Communities

Toledo						Detroit					
1st (86)		2nd (97)		3rd (28)		1st (60)		2nd (102)		3rd (49)	
No.	%	No.	%	No.	%	No.	%	No.	%	No.	%
80	93	71	73	17	61	52	87	54	53	13	26

—although this item is found to be the weakest among the nine convention items.

4. As a symbol of religious pride, the mosque in Toledo has many social and religious functions, one of which is occasionally gathering together the group. Thus Toledo has become more aware than Detroit of the social function of the religious order of Friday noon prayer; it scores much higher on this item than Detroit. Rearranging the convention items in descending order in the three generations within the two communities, we obtain Tables 50 and 51.

A look at Table 50 shows that (1) Detroit's order is closer to the traditional pattern than Toledo's; (2) Toledo in its percentage is higher than Detroit on the total of items; (3) in both communities, the first generation is higher than the second, and the second is higher than the third; (4) general prayer scored the highest in each category. Accepting usury scored the lowest, except in Detroit where it scored higher than Friday noon prayer at the mosque, and except in the third generation of both communities, in contrast with the first and second generations, where it scored higher than Friday noon prayer and pilgrimage. This reveals the same order pattern of Toledo third generation only in contrast with Detroit third generation.

In Toledo's third generation we find strong emphasis on almsgiving (which is a social phenomenon), next in order, following

TABLE 50

Rearrangement of the Convention Items According to the Rank Order of Each Generation in Both Communities

Items of Convention	Generation: *Toledo* 1st	2nd	3rd	*Detroit* 1st	2nd	3rd
Must pray	1	5	5	5	1	1
Must pray five times daily	4	4	1	4	2	7
Must pray at mosque Friday noon	5	1	7	8	5	8
Must fast Ramadan	2	6	8	7	7	4
Must give alms	3	2	4	2	4	2
Must perform pilgrimage	6	3	3	6	8	5
Should not eat pork	7	7	2	1	6	9
Should not drink	8	8	6	3	3	3
Should not accept usury	9	9	9	9	9	6

TABLE 51

Over-all Order of Convention Items, by Community and Generation

Over-all order		COMMUNITY				GENERATION					
	aver-	*Toledo*		*Detroit*		*1st*		*2nd*		*3rd*	
Order	age	Ord.	Ave.	Ord.	Ave.	Ord.	Ave.	Ord.	Ave.	Ord.	Ave.
1	89	1	93	1	85	4	98	1	90	1	83
5	84	5	93	7	82	5	97	5	88	7	77
7	81	4	85	8	79	1	94	2	85	8	73
2	79	6	83	2	78	2	94	4	84	5	66
4	79	7	82	4	77	6	92	7	79	4	62
8	79	2	81	5	75	7	89	6	78	2	59
6	74	3	81	6	65	8	89	3	75	9	53
3	71	8	79	9	63	3	88	8	75	3	51
9	58	9	52	3	62	9	68	9	51	6	50
Average	77		81		74		90		77		64

the religious pattern of the socio-economic middle class, is prayer in general; then follows the prohibition against eating pork and drinking alcohol. Fasting Ramadan is one of the later items, followed by Friday noon prayer at the mosque (due mainly to the pride of the mosque as a religious symbol). Lowest on the scale is the attitude on accepting usury. This low score on interest acceptance matches the general pattern of both communities: the major incentive for the migration to America was the pursuit of wealth and the acquisition of the largest amount of money in the shortest possible time.

5. We observe also that the average score of the Toledo community is higher than the over-all average and correlatively higher than the average of Detroit. Examining the third generation in each community, we find that Detroit's third class is causing the community's lower standard of convention; thus the behavior of this third generation is affecting the degree of the whole community, as shown in Table 48.

The Scale of Religious Knowledge

The religious-knowledge scale is made up of three items:

1. Positive knowledge of ablution before prayer.
2. Positive knowledge of bathing after sexual intercourse.
3. Positive knowledge of the five Islamic Pillars.

Each item of No. 1 and 2 was scored 0 or 1, and the third item was scored 0 or 1 or 2. Those who knew less than two of the five Islamic Pillars scored 0. Those who knew two or three pillars scored 1. And score 2 was given for those who knew more than three pillars.

The scale yielded 5 positions from 0 to 4. These five positions were grouped into three classes: 0 to 1, low; 2, middle; and 3 and 4, high. The distribution of the sample on the scale of knowledge is shown in Table 52.

As was done previously with the component items of the other religious subscales the same procedure is followed here in breaking down this scale by community and generation.

Table 53 shows the following: Toledo is generally higher on the over-all scale of knowledge by the ratio of 58 to 42, and on the average of all items by 63 to 47. Toledo's third generation is higher than Detroit's second generation on the scale of knowledge and on the average of the items. On known ablution, Toledo's third generation is much higher than Detroit's second generation. It can be seen also that Toledo's third generation is higher than its second generation and much higher than Detroit's second generation in knowing the five Islamic pillars.

The table also shows that the contrast is very sharp between the third generation of both communities in religious knowledge. This indicates that *religious knowledge is deteriorating sharply in Detroit while it is reviving in Toledo.* The reason for this will be given in a later stage of analysis. It suffices now to add this point of difference to the ones we previously observed about the third generation in their beliefs and convention.

The Scale of Religious Observances

The manifestation of religiosity appears in religious observances, which is the fourth subscale in our measurement. This subscale is composed of two indices and two items. The indices are

TABLE 52

Distribution of the Sample on the Scale of Religious Knowledge

	High	*Middle*	*Low*	*Total*
No.	220	74	128	422
%	52	18	30	100

TABLE 53

Positive Responses on the Scale of Religious Knowledge and Its Component Items by the Three Generations within the Two Communities

	TOLEDO						DETROIT					
Scale of knowledge and its items	*1st* No.	(86) %	*2nd* No.	(97) %	*3rd* No.	(28) %	*1st* No.	(60) %	*2nd* No.	(102) %	*3rd* No.	(49) %
Over-all scale of religious knowl.	66	77	53	55	12	43	46	77	37	36	6	12
Known ablution	81	94	71	73	19	68	52	87	59	58	22	45
Known bathing after intercourse	74	86	50	52	6	21	48	80	41	40	2	4
Knew four or more of the Islamic pillars	58	67	47	48	15	54	40	67	29	28	6	12
Average		82		58		48		78		42		20

those of abstinence from eating pork and from drinking. The two items are praying and fasting.

Table 54 shows the adherence to each item by the three generations in both communities and reveals the following: (1) Toledo in general is higher than Detroit in these religious practices. (2) The first generation in Detroit is higher than its peer in Toledo, except on fasting. However, the difference on fasting is not significant; it may be very likely due to inaccurate response to the practice questions. This will be mentioned and analyzed later. (3) The third generation in Toledo is higher than the first and second generations on the over-all scale of practice. (4) In praying, the third generation in Toledo is higher than the first and second generations. (5) The Toledo third generation scored higher than the Detroit second and third generations on the over-all scale of practice and in each one of the four components. This again is evidence that Toledo is generally higher than Detroit, and that Toledo's third generation in particular is very much higher than its peer in Detroit.

Table 55 shows the following:

1. Convention within Toledo's three generations is higher than belief. Though slight and apparently insignificant (168 to 163), the difference between them is important for it is indicative of the attitudes of the third generation. While Toledo's other generations scored almost equally on convention and belief, the third generation was more moderate on belief.

2. Toledo's third generation is higher in practice than the first and second generations. There are three reasons for this: the attractive mosque, offering activities that are both religious and social; the highly educated religious leader who has commanded the attention of this youngest generation and, by emphasizing the social functions of religion, obtained the young people's full participation; and the second generation's success in smoothly transmitting to their children the older religious values, thus bridging the expected gap between the first and third generations. Toledo's second generation have oriented their offspring toward religious observance on a rational American basis.

3. The prevailing pattern which characterizes this study of practices is that Toledo within its three generations is higher than Detroit on each item, except where Detroit's first generation shows an insignificant lead over its peer in Toledo.

TABLE 54

Positive Responses on Items of Scale of Practice, by Generation, in Both Communities

	TOLEDO						DETROIT					
	1st	*(86)*	*2nd*	*(97)*	*3rd*	*(28)*	*1st*	*(60)*	*2nd*	*(102)*	*3rd*	*(49)*
	No.	%	No.	%	No.	%	No.	%	No.	%	No.	%
Items of Practice Scale	37	43	28	29	13	46	30	50	15	15	3	6
Subscale: Abstinence from Pork	75	87	72	74	18	64	53	88	65	64	25	51
Subscale: Abstinence from Drinking	58	67	43	44	13	46	46	77	30	29	11	22
Praying at least once a week	45	52	34	35	16	57	41	68	21	21	8	16
Fasting at least 7 days of Ramadan	43	50	30	31	8	29	29	48	15	15	0	0

TABLE 55

Examining the Three Generations in Both Communities on the Four Subscales of Religiosity

a. Total Percentage of Positive Response	b. Percentage of Each Community	c. Total		Religiosity Subscale	Area	Generation 1st		2nd		3rd	
		No.	%			No.	%	No.	%	No.	%
69	39	163	56	Belief	T	79	92	69	71	15	54
	30	130	44		D	53	88	58	57	19	39
68	40	168	59	Convention	T	80	93	71	73	17	61
	28	119	41		D	52	87	54	53	13	27
52	31	131	60	Knowledge	T	66	77	53	55	12	43
	21	89	40		D	46	77	37	37	6	12
30	19	78	62	Practice	T	37	43	28	29	13	46
	11	48	38		D	30	50	15	15	3	6

a. Total percentage of the Sample's positive response on the Religiosity Subscale.
b. Distribution of (a), i.e., the positive response, in percentage, on the two communities.
c. Number and percentage of positive response on the Subscale, in each community.

4. Within each community, the rank order descends from the first to the second to the third generations; the single exception is in Toledo, when the third generation exceeds the first and second generations in practice.

5. The greatest visible contrast between generations appears between the third generations in both communities, especially in knowledge and practice where the ratio is 4 to 1 and 7 to 1 respectively. The ratio of belief to convention is 5 to 3 and 3 to 1.

6. The third generation in Detroit is noticeably much lower, not just than its peer in Toledo, but lower than the first generation in its own community. Unlike Toledo's second generation, the one in Detroit could not bridge the gap between the first and third generations.

Sociological Analyses

As a significant difference is found between the two communities on the four subscales of religiosity and between the religiosity of the third generations in both communities, it is justifiable to conclude that, in general, Toledo is significantly higher in religiosity than Detroit. Whenever we previously observed this difference between the two communities, we tried to discover its associates. In our particular communities we found no significant association between religiosity and sex, between religiosity and occupation, or between religiosity and socio-economic status. Two significant correlations were found, however: between religiosity and generation, and between religiosity and education. To explain the difference in religiosity between the two communities, we tend to link these two significant and independent social variables with the area. Toledo has more first-generation and fewer third-generation members than Detroit; and since the third generation is supposed to be more educated than the second and the first, thus more exposed to the American culture and, by that degree, removed from tradition and religion, we suspected that the main reason for the religious difference between the two communities would lie in the generational composition of the Toledo community, particularly in its having more first-generation and fewer third-generation members than Detroit.

But controlling the other independent social variables and examining the three generations in both communities showed that our original hypothesis was incorrect. The third generation in

Toledo showed a significant difference in religiosity from the third generation in Detroit. Furthermore, the third generation in Toledo showed on many scales a higher degree of religiosity than the second generation, and on one a higher degree than the first. But the generational difference is not significant in its own community; that is, there must be other reasons for this difference in religiosity between our two communities, and we shall now proceed to find them.

Participant observation is one among the many methods used for collecting data for this study. The five months spent in the two communities observing and participating in the intimate social activities of these two communities helped the writer in finding a true clue to this puzzle.

The Social Role of the Second Generation in Both Communities

There is a lack of religious interest as well as community leadership among the second-generation members in Detroit. Despite the fact that the second generation in Detroit is outstripping the first generation in size, we find that the community leadership is still maintained by conservative members of the first generation.

The conservative mentality of those reactionary members, however, rather than provoking a reaction against it, has succeeded in dispersing the interest of both second and third generations—inhibiting them from taking any noticeably active position in community affairs. This dispersion has functioned to disintegrate the community. It has not been a positive disintegration, that is, an assimilation of the values of the host culture. It has been negative, or what Margaret Mead calls "the discontinuity of cultural conditioning." The members of Detroit's second and third generations, by losing interest in their community affairs, have rejected the old values of their own culture and have not modified them or substituted for them by adopting new values of the culture surrounding them. They have developed a marginal attitude whose objective is pluralistic, but often uncertain and ambivalent of community identities.

This dominating behavior of Detroit's first generation immigrants has been transferred from their patriarchal status in the old country. Concentrating ghetto-like in Dearborn, they do not sense the danger of the alien host culture threatening them through their offspring. The older generation never travel farther than from their home to their work. Since their labor occupation does not provide it, they have hardly a chance to get acquainted with the American culture. Furthermore, they have never planned for a long-term policy to prepare for the psychological problems of identification when their offspring would "look for something to identify themselves with in their everyday life," as one first-generation member in Toledo put it. More than 90 per cent of the first-generation members of the Detroit sample admitted that they never planned to establish their lives in America, as illustrated in the following case study.

Case History of a First-Generation Immigrant in Detroit

Our Detroit fellow came to America in 1902. His reasons for leaving his country, Lebanon, or Syria as it was then called, were political and economic. Syria at that time was, among many Middle Eastern countries, a part of the Ottoman Empire whose satellites suffered and bore heavy burdens of political submission, social inferiority to the Turkish ruling class, and economic obligations. Everything was heavily taxed, even one's own garment; no more than one member at a time of the large family could go outside or walk in the street, for the garment had to be sealed to indicate the tax payment.

The main reason for the emigration of our Detroit fellow was the economic misery prevailing in his country. He was 25 years old and mature enough to think of escaping his unhappy fate. He saved a few liras which enabled him to buy his ticket to join some friends on a boat to America in 1902. He did not know where he was going. Knowing no English, he affiliated himself with some Syrian Christians in New York City and followed their occupational pattern of peddling, walking from one state to another. By the end of the year he found himself in another Christian Syrian community in Detroit. He settled down there in 1903 as one of the city's few Moslems. In 1905, he heard of some relatives who had come from Syria and immediately paid them a visit, returning with a 15-year-old wife who during their marriage bore him six children, three boys and three girls.

Our fellow made some money, enough to build his own home, but not enough to go to the old country to show off. He still never thought of establishing his life permanently in America. He bought the house just to save the monthly rent, but was ready to sell it any time he had made enough money to go back with his family. Having been stupified by this dream of collecting enough money and going back to the old country, he neglected to teach his children the instructions of his religion, for "very soon they would learn about their religion back home in Syria," he said pitifully.

The years passed and he found himself engaged in the same kind of job he had had when he first arrived: unskilled labor. One of his two married sons was now divorced from his American wife who claimed the children and brought them up as Christians; his three daughters were married to American, Spanish, and Italian men. He still did not know any more English than a few slang words he heard while peddling and at the factory. In fact, he was never pushed to learn English for he lived in a rapidly growing Arab community. Since his children had married, he no longer saw much of them. Many of his grandchildren married Americans and drifted away from any religious ties they may have had.

Fifty-seven years in America did not change our Detroit fellow much—neither his outlook on life nor his dream of someday returning to the old country to settle there and end his journey. But months after my interview with him, death ended his restless wandering.

The Social Role Played by the Toledo Second Generation

In contrast to Detroit, Toledo second-generation members have played an active role in promoting their children's religious status and in teaching them to be good Moslems and good Americans. Despite the large number of Toledo's first-generation immigrants, these elders have yielded the position of social and religious leadership to the second-generation members who have carried over moderately and very skillfully. After all, they know the different conditions of their present environment and the universal characteristics of their religious heritage. "Islam is not a national religion," said a young second-generation social leader. "It is, rather, international by its unique principles which coincide with general human morals and stress the welfare of society. And," he added, "its details and applications are left to be shaped and reshaped to suit the particular time and place. Islam in America, with its principles, has to take into account the particular features of the American culture. It has to be a living thing in our everyday life and it has to contribute its shares to the culture surrounding us."

Right or wrong in his philosophical religious view, he represents the view of his generation.

Having felt the psychological problems of their children who are looking for something to identify themselves with, the small Moslem community of Toledo in 1955 contributed $80,000 to build one of the newest and most beautiful mosques in the United States. The second generation started the campaign to which the first generation generously contributed.

Since 1955, many second-generation Moslems have moved with their families to Toledo because of the mosque. A young second-generation member bore a heavy loss to move with his family from Virginia to Ohio after the mosque was erected. He said that he wanted his children to be religious and used to send them to church every Sunday in Virginia. Religion to him, springing from a psychological need, helps to solve many everyday problems that are beyond the individual's capacity to solve. In addition, as said before, religion in Toledo is one of the most cherished social values of the middle class, to which the majority of the community belong. The erection of the mosque solved many problems of the second-generation members, especially in providing the necessary religious training for their children.

Being merchants and having wandered through so many states before permanently settling in Toledo, the old-generation members developed a moderate attitude toward sharing the responsibility of community affairs with the second generation. They also accepted the principle of religious coexistence which turned out to work for the best of their interest. As their children expressed the desire to marry Americans, they first advised them to marry from their own people. But when they saw the persistence of their children, they accepted the mixed marriages on the condition that the spouses familiarize themselves with the community affairs, customs, and religion. By this means, the spouse was introduced to the community and studied its religion objectively; and the community, besides keeping its own children, gained new members. It often happened that the American spouses, observing the community's tolerant attitude, converted to Islam and became very active members. By this attitude, the community seems to have violated the traditional religious doctrines which forbid a Moslem girl to marry a non-Moslem. However, there is no explicit prohibition in either the Quran or true tradition against a Moslem girl marrying a follower of a "heavenly Book." It is, however, against the traditions and customs of the old countries that a Moslem girl marry a non-Moslem. The reserved acceptance of Toledo community, therefore, represents a deviation from tradition, tending toward assimilation of the American culture.

The most religiously active members in the Toledo community married outside the faith. They and their spouses have contributed a great deal to the social and religious life of the community. It may be that they have wanted to show the good will and true faith which an ordinary born-Moslem does not need to show. It is also worth mentioning that the Islamic organizations in America, including the Federation of Islamic Associations in the United States and Canada, are the product of the mixed-marriage children.

In conversation with a score of those Moslems who adopted Christianity in both communities, the writer had the impression that they did not do so because of its sound principles or their conviction that Christianity was superior to Islam. The writer was told that the majority of those who became Christians were mostly women in Detroit. They converted out of frustration, having been slighted by the Moslem men who left them to marry Americans. Thus they were forced to marry outside their community and found themselves rejected by their relatives and the entire community. Because of that rejection, they moved away spiritually as well as physically. The Toledo community overcame this problem by absorbing the outsiders into the community.

The high degree of religiosity of the Toledo third generation supports the sociological theory of religious regression. But this regression should not be taken as a general condition for all third generations. Rather, it should be looked at in the light of Merton's "middle range theories," which provide that when the second-generation members carry out the social and religious leadership to bridge the gap between the third and first generations, the third generation then develops a favorable regressional attitude toward the religion of the old generation. Despite this regression, however, the religion of the third generation differs in kind and degree from that of the first.

The religion of the first generation is also associated with nationalistic sentiments. This is the case in Detroit. For this reason, the non-Arab Moslems are not accepted in the community as fully as they are in Toledo. The president of the Youth Organization in Toledo is an Indian Moslem student who is treated and looked upon as a full member of the community. The religious leader is a Yugoslav graduate of al-Azhar University. He is highly respected and fully accepted as a member of the community.

Having searched a very long time for a scholarly religious leader, Detroit was offered the services of that highly educated Toledo religious leader. He was rejected on the grounds of being non-Arab. In his correspondence with the writer, the president of the Detroit community said, "The colony here is trying to contract the Toledo community's sheikh [after he left Toledo]. But the majority, and I am one of them, would rather have a sheikh from Cairo for reasons one of which is [Arab] nationalism."

The Toledo community is, first of all, a *Moslem-American* community. Moslem-oriented, the community recognizes that Islam means more than Arab. It encloses many nations. The religious leader is a non-Arab Moslem. Some Indian students are accepted as full members of the community. The community's sentiment for Egypt or Lybia is a religious sentiment, equal to their feeling toward Indonesia and Pakistan. The horizon of the Toledo community has become as international as Islam itself and not, as in Detroit, confined to Arab nationalism. Being more assimilated into their new environment and farther removed from their old traditions, the members of the Toledo community differentiate between Islam as an international religion and Arab nationalism as a regional political ideology.

Two Sects in the Moslem Communities

The sectarian conflict among the Arab Moslems in Detroit is labeled by two distinct institutions and organizations, the mosque and the club. The mosque is a Sunni institution, with its own sheikh, president, committee, Sunday school, and many other activities.

Many serious incidents have taken place in the Detroit community between these two sects. This conflict has occasionally invited some official religious individuals as well as Arab diplomats to fly from Washington, D.C. to settle it. One can hear about it anywhere in the surrounding Moslem communities; it takes no effort to sense its threat to the unity of the community. Most of the members in Detroit are very sensitive about this conflict and try to hide it by denying that there is any dispute between the Shi'ah and Sunni. A prominent Shi'ah leader wrote, "Your hint at the conflict between Shi'ah and Sunni here surprised me . . . perhaps those who whispered the tone of this [assumed] conflict in your ears did neither help you nor do justice to their brethren here. The necessity for [pure] Islamic work does not leave room for even hinting at the sectarian history and the old incidents that took place between the Moslems in the old times . . . I keep no reservation in saying that the most important reason for diluting the Islamic power lies solely in occupying themselves [the Moslems] with these controversies, Sunni and Shi'ah. . . ." Such an explosive sensitivity reveals a guilty conscience as well as the awareness of the fatal danger of this conflict. But it is doubtful that the rest of the Detroit community is completely aware of this danger.

The conflict does exist in Toledo. But it takes weeks for a keen observer to sense it hidden in the subconscious of the first-generation immigrants, and it is not transferred to the second generation. The ecological dispersion of the community all over the city of Toledo has awakened in the community, especially in the first generation, the sense of religious solidarity lest their children be absorbed by the Christian community.

The ecological conception here is relevant, for it is limited to the spatial and temporal orders of settlement and of institutions. It takes into account the larger society as the effective natural environment in the community life. Thus the community becomes dependent on the larger society to the same degree that the primitive community depends on nature.

The environment of men is not only artificial; it is mental. The world of men is made up of ideas and ideals. Those ideas are the spirit of the community life and constitute its tradition, sentiment, norms, and aspirations. It is these which make up the common mental life. The connection between the ecological system and the values and character of the peoples can be very clearly seen from the distinct types of urban and rural modes of life. It can also be seen in the numerous forms of social institutions in different societies.

In the light of human ecological theory, the difference in the degree of religiosity between the Toledo and Detroit communities is the function of the location and position of each community within the larger society. The Toledo community is scattered all over the city. This dispersion helps the community to achieve a high degree of assimilation. Secular or social religion is one of the characteristics of the American middle class. The majority of the Moslem community, falling into the socio-economic middle class, tend to acquire that religious characteristic.

But if they are proud of being Americans because of the wealth and social standard they have achieved, which the original country could not offer them, we can conclude that nationality is not as strongly identical with ego as is religion. Nationality is very much more recent in the history of man than religion. Hence religion has deeper roots in the psychological make-up of man. Man may change everything—his clothes, his name, his habits of dress and food, his language and his nationality—but not with the same degree of ease may he change his religion. Religion, even social religion, is identical with one's entity and is the last pride of man. The dispersion of the members of the Toledo community awakened their sense of the danger of their children being absorbed by the predominant Christian culture. The community's sense of this danger has functioned to liquidate the existing sectarian conflict in such a way as to strengthen the Islamic solidarity as a religious fort to defend the community faith and belief. The American principle of religious freedom, along with the religious characteristics of the socio-economic middle class, has encouraged the Islamic movement in the community; the movement has gained more social prestige and become a distinguished religious community very highly respected by the larger society. The second and third generations in Toledo know very little about Sunni and Shi'ah. They are all just Moslems—American Moslems.

In Detroit, however, one may hear the second and third generations talking seriously about their sectarian conflict as if it were between Catholics and Protestants. In her interview, a second-generation woman did not forget to mention the merits of the Shi'ah in contrast to Sunni. Her American sister-in-law was present and asked the writer the reasons for that sectarian conflict. She pointed out that she did not even know to which sect her husband belonged (because of disinterest in community affairs—the general prevailing pattern in Detroit). The interviewee interfered angrily, stating that her husband belonged to the Shi'ah club and not to the Sunni mosque.

To reemphasize: the concentration of the Detroit community into a single section in Dearborn has helped transfer the complete social atmosphere of the old country to the new world. That Arabic atmosphere has blinded the community's eyes to the alien culture by which they are surrounded. Insensible to the surrounding religious impact which is squeezing the community and negatively gaining those whom the community rejects, such as the Moslem girl who marries an American, the Detroit community is very weak in its religious solidarity. But does this hasten the process of assimilation in the Detroit community as compared to the Toledo community? Our data and statistical evidence answer this negatively.

America as a Melting Pot of Nations

At the ceremony of naturalization of American citizenship, one is told not to be a hyphenated American. "From now on, you are not British-American, Italian-American, or French-American. You are just American." This is what is meant by "America is a nation of nations." The first step in the process of assimilation is assuming that attitude of being hyphenated American. The final step is the feeling of being not hyphenated American but only American. The continuum of the assimilation scale has the two radical ends: one feels pure American or one still feels a part of the old nation.

There is no objection, from the point of view of naturalization, to being Christian-American or Moslem-American, or whatever religion one chooses. Religious freedom is, after all, one of the most cherished freedoms in America.

Contrary to what we suspected before testing the communities —that their different generational compositions caused their differences in religiosity—the Toledo third generation is higher in religiosity than the second. This condition supports the sociological theory of religious regression. Toledo's third generation is also very much higher in religiosity than Detroit's third generation.

It was pointed out above that the kind of religion in Toledo differs from that in Detroit. The latter is traditional, with sectarian features, while the former is Americanized and stresses the more general religious principles more strongly than the particular Islamic features. This is due to the social and religious roles played by the second generation in Toledo which have utilized some American religious values and introduced them into their religion.

It is advocated here that there is no negative correlation between religiosity and assimilation. Toledo is more assimilated than Detroit in the American culture; yet, as we established statistically, it is more religious. No attempt is made here to trace the causation. It suffices for our purpose to establish the correlation.

Some American Values

At a formal meeting of the American Muslim Society of Toledo, held at the new mosque, the president proposed to the committee the introduction of the bingo game at the mosque as a possible source of support. Although the proposal did not pass, its very introduction indicates the direction in which the community is moving as well as its degree of assimilation of certain values of the host culture.

That most of the Toledo male members are owners of bars, alcoholic beverage stores, and liquor-licensed restaurants is another evidence of assimilation. Although within the realm of religious practice the people are firm on abstinence from drinking, they have made an occupational shift from traditional values to a new set of values. During Ramadan, the writer often had interviews with members of the community at their bars while he found them fasting. The beautiful mosque, the most striking religious institution in the community, is built from liquor money. Paradoxically, the shift in occupational values has helped to sustain the religious institution.

Could it be that the subconscious religious guilt is sublimated by generous material support to the religious institutions? While satisfying their religious conscience, the Toledo members also show the surrounding Moslem communities how religiously well the liquor trader's community is. As businessmen have no limited ceiling on their earnings, the members of the Moslem community in Toledo believe that the more they give for the support of their religious institutions, the more they will earn and their earning will become blessed and purified from the sin of its means. It is a kind of religious reconciliation with the deity, in which flourishing social functions are associated with the process of assimilation. Religious movements throughout history have owed a great deal to the consciousness of sin, perhaps even more than to the feeling of piety. The pious man very often lives on the secular contribution offered by the sinner. The pious, traditional first generation of Detroit have not contributed to the religious movement as much as to the cause of Arab nationalism, whereas the occupationally deviant Toledo first generation have contributed more to the cause of Islam than to Arab nationalism.

As the feeling of nativity is one measure of assimilation, we measured those who considered themselves Arab-Americans against those who felt pure American. The results are shown as percentages of the total number of each generation in both communities (Table 56).

We observe that the process of Americanization is working in both communities cross-sectionally and correlated with generation. Second, the process is faster and deeper in Toledo's first and second generations than in their peer generations in Detroit. Third, the process of assimilation is generally deeper in Toledo than in Detroit, and is particularly deeper among Toledo's third generation than among its peer generation in Detroit, by the ratio of 71 to 64. The difference between the two communities, however, is not statistically significant and in fact refutes the prevailing theory that adherence to the traditional religion has a negative correlation with assimilation.

Friday Noon Prayer in Both Communities

The Moslem weekly holiday is Friday. Friday noon prayer at the mosque, observed in the Arab and Moslem countries, has the social and religious importance of Sunday services at the Christian churches. It is still observed in our two American communities, although in different degrees.

Who Attends Friday Noon Prayer at the Mosque

In general, the number of those who attend Friday noon prayer in the two communities is small. It is relatively much smaller in Detroit than in Toledo. In the latter, an average of 18 persons, one-third of whom are second-generation members of both sexes, attend the weekly prayer; in Detroit less than 10 persons attend, all of whom are first-generation male. When we consider that

TABLE 56
Feeling of Nativity

	TOLEDO			DETROIT		
	1st	*2nd*	*3rd*	*1st*	*2nd*	*3rd*
Arab-American	22	61	29	17	59	36
American	7	28	71	3	24	64
Total	29	89	100	20	83	100

the Toledo community is one-fifth the size of the Detroit community, we may conclude that Friday noon attendance is observed at the mosque in Toledo and Detroit by the ratio of 9 to 1. Although it has more retired and unemployed persons with no deterrent to their observation of that ritual practice, the Detroit community had no regular respectable religious leader. Their religious leader, not an *imam*, but a volunteer sheikh, had a limited degree of self-education, despite the weekly Arabic newspaper which he publishes in Detroit. All religious activities performed by him were on a voluntary basis. When he did not go to the mosque, because of sickness, out-of-town marriage or funeral ceremonies, the Friday noon prayer was suspended.

In Toledo as well as in Detroit, the Friday noon prayer follows the traditional way: some verses from the Quran are recited; then a speech in Arabic is given by the religious leader, followed by a group prayer.

Sunday Activities as a Sign of Americanization

While we observed no change at all from the traditional conduct of Friday noon prayer, we find a great change from traditions on Sunday. In fact, Sunday with its activities provides us with a good measurement for assimilation. Therefore, these activities will be dealt with in detail, to see whether one community is more religiously active and thus more integrated with the American culture than the other. This leads us to ask a question: Has one community become more *Sunday religious* than the other? From what we have seen—that the Detroit community is much less active on Friday than Toledo—we may suspect that it is more religiously active on Sunday. We may answer our question by examining the religious activities of the three generations in both communities in the light of 1) Sunday school, and 2) Sunday noon prayer.

Sunday School in Detroit

There is practically no Sunday school at all at the mosque, with the exception of a lecture given each Sunday in the basement by a volunteer first-generation member who speaks fair English. Those who attend are about ten women, half of whom are old ladies who understand no English, and, on the average, no more than one first-generation male. It was said that the lecturer did not know how to attract the younger generation by dealing with modern subjects that touch their everyday lives—their problems and status in this country, how to conform with their religious background to this alien surrounding, and so forth. The Sunday noon prayer, led by the previously described self-semi-educated religious leader, is quietly attended by four or five old-generation members.

Besides the Detroit mosque, there is the Hashimite Club which is regarded in the community as a Shi'ah institution. There are two large active Sunday schools in this club, one for religious instructions and one for the Arabic language. Table 57 shows the grades of the religious school, along with the number listed in each class according to age.

All classes are held on the second floor. Grades 1 and 2 are conducted simultaneously in two big separate rooms by two second-generation women; Grade 3 is conducted by a second-generation young man in the big hall where prayer is held. The classes last from 11 A.M. to noon, at which time the students attend Sunday noon prayer. As the students of Grades 1 and 2 take off their shoes and line up, waiting for the *Mu'thin* (one who calls for the prayer) to finish, they do not perform ablution since the prayer is given in the form of a lesson.

The call for prayer is performed by one of the students. Except for a small sentence inserted after "Hayy'ala as-slah" and before "Qad Qamat as-salah" (the sentence is "Hayy ila kheir el-'amal"—"hurry to perform the best work"), is otherwise identical with the traditional wording. The prayer is led by a student from Grade 2. He recites the prayer loudly and is followed by the rest of the students.

TABLE 57

Sunday School in Detroit, by Grades and Age Distribution

Grade	*Age*	*No.*	*Curricula*
1	4-6	60	Stories from the Quran about the prophets
2	7-10	60	Teaching prayers and short surah from the Quran
3	11 and over	40	Current religious events and their social significance

Indeed, the Shi'ahs in Detroit have a zealous sense of religiosity. The proportion of their educated is much higher than that of the Sunnis. They are more socially and religiously active, and for this they are resented by the Sunnis who accuse them of having caused a serious split in the community. The Sunnis want to maintain the social and religious leadership in the community, although they are not capable of doing so. The increasing religious activities by the Shi'ahs are met with increasing nationalistic Arab activities by the Sunnis. There is only limited cooperation between the two groups within communities in these two procedures.

Sunday School in Toledo

Sunday is not the only active day in the Toledo mosque. There are many activities every day: at least one religious group comes daily from different religious faiths and institutions to acquaint themselves with their Moslem fellow citizens; there are occasional meetings and parties; at certain times one is always sure to meet the religious leader of the community in the mosque. Nevertheless, Sunday is the most active day of the week in the regular life of the mosque. It is the day of Sunday school and practically every family brings its children to the school to learn about their religion. There are about 150 students enlisted in the school, ranging in age from 4 to over 15. The five classes, along with their distribution according to age, are presented in Table 58.

The curriculum is very well organized and harmonized by the religious leader who arranges the lessons weekly and meets with the teachers beforehand to instruct them on how to conduct the

TABLE 58

Sunday School in Toledo, by Grades and Age Distribution

Grade	*Age*	*No.*	*Curricula*
1	15+	80	Islamic history and philosophy
2	10-14	15	Religious practices with their social significance
3	7-9	15	Basic Islamic pillars and beliefs
4	4-6	40	Simple religious stories about the prophets
5	Parents	90	Religious ethics from traditions

lessons. Toward the end of the year, these lessons are collected to be followed in Sunday school in the years to come. The teachers are exclusively second-generation young women, some of whom are the product of mixed marriages.

The four small classes start in the basement from 10:00 A.M. until 11:30; the fifth, conducted by the sheikh, is held upstairs from 11:30 to noon. This arrangement is to give the religious leader a chance to supervise the classes. In return, it gives the teachers and older children a chance to hear lectures about Islamic ethics. All the classes and lectures are given in English. About noon, all the attendants, from three generations, are engaged in the Sunday noon prayer, lining up behind the religious leader in a traditional way; females are at the end of the group. After the classes and lecture, there is a collection. This collection has the function of teaching the youth how to support their mosque. It is also a borrowed element from the American churches.

Chanting the prayer loudly at Sunday noon is a kind of adjustment to the American environment. Its practical function is to teach the youth how to perform prayer. Sunday noon prayer itself, as it is done in the Toledo community, represents a kind of over-all religious integration with the American environment. It fills the religious vacuum in the spirit of those youths who see their friends and schoolmates belonging and going to a church of which they are proud. Now, they too have a God to fill their entity, to Whom they bow and kneel, and from Whose unlimited power they derive their power to conquer problems of everyday life. The mosque institution plays a vital role in the life of the entire community, for religion's vital psychological functions integrate the individual personality with that of the surrounding society.

There is also an Arabic school held every Thursday evening at the mosque from 7 to 8:30. This school has three classes, with the following distribution:

TABLE 59

Arabic School in Toledo, by Grades and Age Distribution

Class	*No. of Students*	*Age of Students*
1	15	Adults, 17+
2	10	10-16
3	25	5-9

The Arabic language is an inseparable part of Islam. As the religious leader puts it, "It is a must for all Moslems to know some Arabic . . . for religious reasons." This is the prevailing pattern in the community. Arabic language as well as Arabic activities are employed to serve the religious goals. The community's emphasis is on religion. Occasionally, some Arab diplomats are invited to help raise the social prestige of the Moslem community (see the Toledo *Blade*, December 6, 1958).

The mosque institution in Toledo has three separate branches and organizations:

Men's Branch	120 members meet once a month on Sunday
Women's Auxiliary	60 members meet twice a month on Wednesday
Youth Club	40 members meet twice a month on Monday

The Toledo Youth Organization is under the Islamic Youth Association, which is sponsored by the Islamic Federation. The Toledo Youth Organization issues a monthly paper, edited and printed in the Toledo mosque, for all the Youth Organizations in the United States and Canada.

Comparison between the Two Communities in Religiosity

As we have observed the difference in degree of religiosity between the two communities, and have seen that Toledo in general is higher than Detroit, we noticed a striking difference in the degree of the religiosity between the third generation in both communities. This difference is the result of multi-variables:

1. The selectivity, in Toledo, of the first-generation members who established the community after many years of wandering from one state to another. That period of traveling exposed them to the American culture and developed in them new values which modified their attitudes. For example, they tolerate mixed marriages for their girls. By this tolerant attitude they have kept the members of their community and gained some foreign elements which have helped to cultivate the traditional values so as to suit the new social environment.

2. The ecological distribution of the community in Toledo has awakened them to the possible danger of being absorbed by the alien, prevailing religion. This fear of the visible danger has solidified the community by melting its sectarian differences.

3. Toledo's second generation has played a vital role in bridging the gap between the first and third generations, who both show a strong religious adherence.

4. The kind of religion in Toledo is moderate, with the stress on general religious elements rather than on the specific Islamic features. Because of this moderation, it has suited the new social environment and been capable of attracting the third generation with its American outlook.

5. The religion of the Toledo community is purely social, similar to that of the American middle class. Arabic elements in Toledo are means and not the end.

6. The community's religion is more Sunday than Friday religion. The Toledo community is a Moslem American community which will carry Islam from one generation to another and diffuse it among those foreign elements which have entered the community through its moderate attitude toward the vital problem of mixed marriage.

In contrast with Toledo, the first-generation members of the Detroit community, having come directly to Detroit from the old country, have maintained unmodified their old values.

1. They cannot tolerate their female children's mixed marriages. When the girls have not found Moslem boys, they have married Americans, to find themselves and their offspring rejected by the community.

2. Living in isolation in Dearborn, they have not sensed the impact of the surrounding religious danger. Among the traditional values they have maintained is the social conflict between Shi'ahs and Sunnis. This conflict over social leadership has weakened the solidarity of the community and dispersed the religious interest of the young generations.

3. As a result, the second generation in its religious apathy have not transmitted the sense of religiosity to the third generation, which shows a very weak sense of religiosity.

4. Detroit's religion is still traditional and rigid; it may not suit the new social environment or cannot attract the American-minded third generation.

5. The religion is used as a means to nationalistic sentiments, maintained by the old generation and lost in meaning among the third generation.

6. The religion is more a Friday religion which is beginning to fade even among the first generation. It will not find strong carriers unless it is modified to suit the new environment and unless it can attract the younger generations. This does not mean that there is a negative correlation between religiosity and Arab nationalistic sentiments. But keeping religion traditional, as Detroit has done, has weakened its structure in the new world. By losing religion, the sense of Arabism will be completely lost. Some skillful modification is needed—modification which will increase the younger generation's religiosity in harmony with their position as good Moslem Americans. In this harmony, they will work toward bettering the mutual understanding between the two worlds, among different religions, and, above all, within their own religious leadership.

7. A great deal of the difference between the two communities' degree of religiosity is attributable to the personalities of their religious leaders. The Toledo community has a highly educated religious leader with a respectable social personality. He devotes most of his time to the mosque activities for the sake of the community and the larger society. The community pays him full-time wages and, in turn, gains his full and sincere services. The Detroit community lacks such religious leadership. The education of the volunteer religious leader can by no means be compared with that of Toledo's religious leader; his personality, too, suffers by comparison. However educated Detroit's second religious leader, the Shi'ah imam, may be, he is without religious flexibility and is not very popular among many Shi'ahs and most of the Sunnis.

In addition, both sheikhs in Detroit are said to take advantage of their community by collecting as much money as they can from the members. The community, which trusts neither sheikh, does not pay them; thus the leaders charge every individual for their religious services. Where Toledo's religious leader sheds respect on the whole community, that office is still empty in Detroit.

8. In Toledo, the latent function of the occupational pattern—most, as we have seen, are engaged in the liquor business—has been to stir up religious consciousness as a reaction to the members' feelings of guilt. Those who feel they are sinners contribute much more to religious activities than those who feel pious. Those

who assume the role of the pious and the saints often live on their religion. The traditional community of Detroit, on the other hand, does not need to compensate through religion for any serious kind of religious deviation. Feeling, with their sin, the uncertainty of all business people and the dependence on hope for future financial betterment, the people of Toledo are motivated to strengthen their relations with God; from Him they expect forgiveness as well as reciprocal secular reward.

Hoping to compensate for their sin by using it as a means to increase their secular reward and social status and prestige, and hoping to be thought religious by a society which respects religiosity—these are the motivations for Toledo's religiosity. Toledo's spectacular adherence to this norm shows adequate adjustment to the increasing secular emphasis of both time and space.

CHAPTER SIX

The Two Communities Compared

The Arab Moslems first migrated to the United States in large numbers at the turn of the twentieth century, at least one generation after the Arab Christians came. Religion was the chief factor delaying the Moslems in their migration to the American Christian world. Economic factors—poor socio-economic conditions in the old countries and prosperous economic expansion in the new world—caused their migration. They did not intend to establish themselves permanently in the United States, but wanted to accumulate the most money possible in the shortest time and then return home.

Though attracted to America, they were handicapped by their lack of knowledge of English. They therefore encountered many difficulties and did not find the rosy picture they had been given of America. By the time they overcame the linguistic problem, they had achieved a degree of social adjustment and found themselves with families and American-born children. Torn between the memories of the old countries and the prosperity they were enjoying in the new country, between their desire to go back and the persistence of their children to remain in America, the Arab Moslems made a compromise: to remain in America and maintain an equilibrium between their two cultures. Islam was their most cherished cultural element and they strove to keep it in the new culture. But the flood of assimilation threatened to sweep away the old cultural elements, including Islam.

This book has examined the hypothesis of a negative correlation between the strength of religion and rapidity of assimilation into a new culture. For this purpose, two communities in the same geographical region were studied: the Arab-Moslem communities in Toledo, Ohio, and Detroit, Michigan.

The Social Structure of Each Community

Toledo

As we have related, the Moslem community first entered the liquor business by accident, then by imitation. It happened that one of the first settlers "fell into this business accidentally," as he put it, and found it profitable. To secure maximum profit with minimum cost, he imported from other states some of his relatives to help him expand the business. These business-minded relatives shortly branched out and started their own bars, motivated by the desire to imitate the successful relative. The same story was repeated several times, thus shaping the occupational pattern of the majority of the community.

Toledo's occupational pattern reveals two significant points. First, assimilation itself leads to the possibility of certain occupational patterns. Toledo Moslems would not have dared to choose the traditionally condemned liquor business had they not assimilated the new values and adjusted themselves to the American culture. This leads to the second significant point: selectivity. The members who came to Toledo were selective groups from among the Arab Moslems who were scattered all over the United States. Selectivity here means that the liquor business attracted to Toledo a special class of Moslems—those characterized by readiness to sacrifice some traditional values. In the Detroit community the very opposite condition—the persistence of tradition—has prevented any of its first-generation members from emulating the Toledo community.

Detroit

The occupational pattern of the Detroit community follows the general pattern of the non-English-speaking immigrant groups from East Europe and Asia: The majority of Detroit members are unskilled workers who found an easy, profitable line of work in the city's auto industry. Such work does not require special skills, nor does it significantly increase one's need to assimilate. Moreover, the occupational pattern of the Detroit Arab Moslems furnished the basis for their concentration in Dearborn, near the Ford plant. The forces of social change thus lost the effective weapon of language, for the factory workers found little occasion to learn English at work, where communication was at a minimum, or at home, where the Moslems lived a segregated life. The

Detroit first-generation members have remained typical traditionalists and preserved many old values, some of which have disappeared in the changing home countries themselves. Among the traditional values retained in Detroit is the patriarchal family structure. This follows the division of labor in the less advanced agrarian societies, where the heaviest administrative burden rests on the head of the family. Every member of the family has to participate in a subsistence economy: the head assigns a particular task to each member, thus coordinating family effort.

This traditional attitude carried over to the new world by the Detroit first generation has further implications in the social structure of community life. It magnifies the conflict between the first generation and the American-born second generation. This conflict is manifested particularly in the community leadership. Despite the small ratio of the first to the second generation in Detroit, the members of the first generation dominate the community and do not give way to the second generation's participation in community leadership. This attitude of the older generation has fostered an apathetic response from the second generation concerning the community social affairs; thus, due to the uncompromising outlook of both generations, the process of assimilation has been reduced.

The Ecological Distribution

Detroit

The traditional attitude retained by Detroit's first generation is exhibited in the ecological location of the Moslem community. The majority of the community are concentrated in the ghetto-like area of Dearborn. Linguistic and occupational factors contributed to this residential pattern. The Syrian grocery stores, the coffeehouses, and the Arab atmosphere almost isolate the community from the American society and thus the cultural influence of the adopted country is reduced. The American cultural elements and values carried by the American-born young generations are hardly absorbed by the old generation. And the compulsory educational system in America has only widened the cultural gap between the two generations.

Detroit's new generation has learned a different language which carries different symbols and values from those of the old generation. They mix with Americans in their play and school and are thus fully exposed to the American culture. But the rigid attitude of the old generation at home and in the community has prevented the establishment of an equilibrium between the two cultures in the single generation who are bearers of both: the generation born in America. Diffusion of American values in the Detroit community has been minimized by the patriarchal attitude of the first generation, in addition to the residential concentration. The second generation, despite their large numbers, find themselves voiceless. Resentful and confused, they have been blocked from adjusting to either culture and have thus emerged in a cultural vacuum or discontinuity. These American cultural values which have been internalized by the American-educated second generation have not found overt outlets in the Dearborn community. With the cultural discontinuity, that suppression of internalized values has contributed to the molding of the second generation's marginal personality.

Toledo

The peculiar residential pattern of the Toledo community worked out, paradoxically, to provide a high degree of social harmony between the first and second generations. It was expected that the residential concentration in Detroit would bridge the generational gap; instead, it widened the gulf. In contrast, the residential scattering of the Toledo community might be expected to have alienated the second generation from the first. But on the contrary, it strengthened the generational ties as well as the community identification. The first-generation members, residentially dispersed in the larger society, were more exposed to the American culture whose open-class system invited them to acquire the social habits of the American middle class. With no physical characteristics to distinguish them from the Americans, the Toledo first-generation immigrants were acculturated as soon as they solved the linguistic problem. The linguistic adjustment came as a result of intimate contact with the larger society in business as well as in residence. The Moslems acted and interacted within the American social framework. They imitated and acquired the American behavior in their family and community relations with the second generation.

One of the most important products of the American influence on the Toledo first generation has been the shift from a patriarchal family toward an equalitarian family and community. Community leadership was voluntarily handed over by the first to the second generation. Because of this freely given legacy, the second generation became interested in the community affairs. To maintain the delicate equilibrium between its religio-ethnic background and its new American status, this generation embraced a religious rather than national outlook. This was a natural and comfortable process, for religion in America is the apparent characteristic of the middle class. The residential dispersion of the community gave the second generation two alternatives: either convert to Christianity or modify Islam to function in the new environment. Since religion is an important factor in Moslem life, and since the Moslems quickly learned that separate religious identification is tolerated in a multi-group democracy, the second generation took the second alternative. This religious attitude of the second generation was met with appreciation by the first, increasing the degree of the community trust to the second.

The accommodation between the two generations helped to stabilize the modal personality of the Toledo second generation. Moreover, it adjusted ethical and social principles in Islam to solidify the community's identity within the American society. Hence the phase of the background nationality, Arab, was isolated from the general concept of Islam. This attitude was concretely expressed, moreover, when the community employed a non-Arab religious leader. The residential dispersion which had weakened the nationality background also weakened the traditional sectarian conflict. The ratio of Shi'ahs to Sunnis in Toledo is similar to that in Detroit. But more exposure to the adopted culture in Toledo diffused the sectarian identification and strengthened the religious structure of the unified community. The second generation looks at the community as a Moslem American community without hyphenation. Its religious behavior, it feels, conforms to the American pattern and is thus an evidence of assimilation. Having committed themselves to permanent settlement in America, the Toledo first-generation members welcomed the moderate attitudes of their children, who increased their knowledge not only of American life but also of Islam.

The Time of Settlement

Despite its relatively short history, the Moslem community in Toledo has achieved a higher degree of assimilation than the older Detroit community. Although settlement is not an accurate measurement of the time variable (for the majority of the Toledo families did not come directly from the old countries to the community but, rather, migrated from other states), the time variable could be measured by the year of emigration from the old countries as well as by the number of generations born in America in each community. Both measures were used, and it was found that Detroit community was older than Toledo. Consequently, it was expected that Detroit would be more assimilated than Toledo. But the ecological factors—residential concentration in Detroit and dispersion in Toledo—have outweighed the differences in time. Persistence of traditional ethnic traits has been maximized in Detroit by the residential concentration as well as by the large size of the community; it has been minimized in Toledo by the residential dispersion as well as by the small size of the community.

Assimilation

Occupational as well as residential differences may affect the degree of assimilation in both communities. Commerce by its nature involves human interaction, while the nature of labor, in this age of automation is to involve more human isolation. For this reason, Detroit's occupational pattern has impeded the processes of assimilation. The majority of the Toledo community, however, is engaged in business on the level of owners and managers. Success in business depends, to a large degree, on social skills in conversation and good relations with the clients. When the business is liquor and the clients are Americans, the social circle between the ethnic Arab community and the adopted American culture is naturally completed. The liquor business pattern indicates the predisposition of the Toledo Moslems to shift from traditions to new values. It is a sign of readiness to go along the way of assimilation.

Selectivity

The variable of selectivity accounts for Toledo community's deviation in occupational patterns. The liquor business attracted to Toledo, as we have seen, a special class of Moslems whose personal elasticity was the favorable soil for the seeds of assimilation. These people, long before they settled in Toledo, had acquired flexibility in wandering from one state to another and thus being exposed to the American culture.

The liquor business in Toledo did not attract any of the first-generation members of the adjacent community of Detroit. Those very few from Detroit who were attracted were from the second generation. The traditional Detroit personality is not willing to engage in the occupational pattern of Toledo. Even the majority of the second-generation members, some of whom may drink, dislike the Toledo community because of its liquor pattern; these members are under the influence of traditional values.

Social Leadership

The small ratio of the Detroit's old generation to the second and third generations indicates the decline of the first generation. But despite this, the first generation still maintains community leadership which reduces their motivation to assimilation. Barred from handling community affairs, the Detroit second-generation members cannot introduce significant changes into the community. They can neither adhere to the traditional values of the dominant first generation nor find a way legitimately to practice in the community what they have internalized through the American educational media. They have found their outlets in outside activities which add very little to the community life.

In contrast, the ratio of the first generation in Toledo to the second and third generations is much higher than that in Detroit. But the previously mentioned factors (business occupation, residential dispersion, selectivity, and elastic personality) have allowed the Toledo first generation to give way to the second in managing the community affairs. If the Detroit community represents a tradition's struggle to continue its way in a strange environment, the Toledo community may be seen as an initiation of social cultivation. The expert members are allowed to do the job. Those experts are the second-generation members. They invest their time and efforts in promoting the community prestige, for they feel it is their community. The difference between the two communities is the product of the attitudes of their second generations. These attitudes, in turn, reflect upon the position of each community's third generation. While the third generation in both communities have achieved an identical high degree of assimilation, the Toledo third generation shows a regressional attitude toward the Islamic practice, as shown in Table 60.

On the scale of religious practice, Toledo's third generation exceeded the second and even the first generation. Except on the item of abstinence from eating pork, where the decline continued from the second to the third by 74 to 64 per cent, this religious regression is the general pattern in Toledo. However, 64 per cent is the identical percentage in the Detroit second generation.

The Detroit third generation is leaving the religious values of the community. This is, as we have seen, because the generational gap is not bridged by the second generation. There is a social vacuum in Detroit between the American third and the traditional first generation. The passive attitude of the Detroit second generation has deprived the community of the ethnic transitional institution which is skillfully retained in Toledo by the second generation. The influence of the active role played by the Toledo second generation on the third can be seen in the area of religious organization membership: 32 per cent of the third generation are active members in the religious organization, in contrast to 4 per cent of the Detroit third. Religious organization in Toledo is the modern institution of the equalitarian community; in Detroit it is the traditional institution of the patriarchal first generation. Social activities introduced to the religious organization by the Toledo second generation have stimulated the effort of the youth to satisfy their desires to be good American Moslems, while in Detroit traditional concepts of religious organization have driven away the youth who found themselves in a state of conflict between their desires to be simultaneously American and Arab.

Religious Leadership

Such a state of conflict is accentuated in Detroit by the sectarian dispute between Sunnis and Shi'ahs. In their struggle for social leadership and in the absence of second generation influence, each sect tries to derive its social power from greater adherence to Arab nationalism in the old countries. As a result, religion in Detroit became mixed with nationalism. Religious leaders there are ambitious laymen whose concerns are with wealth; they have lost the esteem and respect of the Detroit youth

In Toledo, however, certain aspects of the religion enable the community to fulfill a social function: identification with Ameri-

TABLE 60

*Positive Response on Religious Practices by Generations within Each Community**

	TOLEDO						DETROIT					
	1st	(86)	*2nd*	(97)	*3rd*	(28)	*1st*	(60)	*2nd*	(102)	*3rd*	(49)
Religious Practices	No.	%	No.	%	No.	%	No.	%	No.	%	No.	%
Scale of Religious Practice	37	43	28	29	13	46	30	50	15	15	3	6
Abstinence from Pork	75	87	72	74	18	64	53	88	65	64	25	51
Abstinence from Drinking	58	67	43	44	13	46	46	77	30	29	11	22
Praying	45	52	34	35	16	57	41	68	21	21	8	16
Fasting	43	50	30	31	8	29	29	48	15	15	0	0

* The difference, as measured by χ^2, is found significant at a level of .02.

ca's socio-economic middle class. The scholarly religious leader in Toledo made the mosque the center of social activities and it became the natural liaison between the community and the larger society. The many religious activities on American social levels have left no room for the sectarian dispute. Both sects are pursuing a new social position in a new environment and they have realized that they cannot achieve it without cooperation; for they do not seek the new position through rigid traditions or political affiliation with the old country, but rather by adherence to the criteria of the class to which they aspire. The non-Arab identity of the religious leader has also contributed to the sectarian cooperation and solidarity. The sectarian division is connected in the minds of those people with regional divisions in the old countries. It is used, they feel, to stimulate social and political support in the absence of deep ideological feeling. *Being non-Arab, the religious leader is not suspected of being partial toward one of the two sects;* thus religion functions on a purely Islamic level. The difference in religious leadership of the two communities is one of the strongest factors in accounting for the difference in their religiosity as well as assimilation. The great majority of those second-generation members in both communities who are religious were found to have learned about their religion from the mosque rather than from their parents. And the lack of a respected, scholarly religious leader in Detroit was found to be responsible for the community's religious ignorance as well as their lower degree of both religiosity and assimilation. The higher degree of religiosity of Toledo could be accredited to the efforts of its religious leader.

Interreligious Marriage

The difference in each community's attitude toward interreligious marriage accounts, in part, for their differences in degree of assimilation: 31 per cent in Toledo, in contrast to 46 per cent in Detroit, oppose the interreligious marriage. Although this kind of marriage is actually more practiced in Detroit than in Toledo (by a small margin—25 per cent in Detroit to 20 per cent in Toledo), the negative attitude in Detroit has brought it a heavy loss in its women. Detroit does not tolerate its young women who marry Americans even if the Americans, as a matter of expediency, adopt Islam. Though there are no statistics, the Detroit community is aware that a great number of Moslem girls have left the community and adopted Christianity to give their rejected children a religious identification.

In accordance with the tolerant attitude developed in Toledo toward interreligious marriage, the American spouses gained by the community have increased the community's degree of assimilation and produced a cultivated American Moslem generation. The American members are accepted and found to be very active in the community's religious affairs.

Recapitulation

This study was made to discover the variables associated with the difference in the degree of assimilation and religiosity between two communities of identical religio-ethnic background. These are the Arab Moslem communities in Toledo, Ohio, and Detroit, Michigan.

Contrary to what was expected, assimilation worked hand in hand with religiosity; that is, the higher in religiosity, the more assimilated the community is to the American society. The Toledo community, in contrast to the Detroit community, possesses these two characteristics. But the kind of religion in Toledo was found to be different from that of Detroit. Both communities adhere to the Islamic faith. But some modifications have entered into the religion of Toledo. The religious characteristics of Toledo are: (a) more activities on Sunday than on Friday, (b) more emphasis on social activity than pure faith, (c) leniency in traditional belief, and (d) rationalism, that is, more Americanization. Detroit's religion is characterized by the following: (a) less Sunday activity, (b) ritualism, (c) rigidity, and (d) dogmatism—that is, it is more traditional.

The differences in religion are the result of different religious media and carriers. Religious activities are carried in Toledo by the second generation, while in Detroit they are still held by the first generation, despite the fact that the proportion of first-generation members in Detroit is much smaller than in Toledo.

The persistence of the Detroit first generation in the community leadership is associated with its traditional patriarchal attitudes which have lessened the community's degree of assimilation. In addition, this traditional patriarchal attitude in community affairs has discouraged the interest of the Detroit second generation, which therefore play a passive role. They could neither Americanize Islam to fit into the new social environment nor find traditional views or religion appealing in their age of secularization.

In the Toledo community, the religious leader plays a dual role in conformity with what the second generation expect from him. In the religious area he deals with Islam in his teaching, lecturing, and writing on a high level of generalization, stressing that its general ethical principles of humanity are not monopolized by any nation or any race. This has enabled the Toledo Moslems to live peacefully side by side with Americans of different religions. This adaptability of the Toledo Moslems has increased mutual understanding between the community and the larger surrounding society, and as a result has enhanced the prestige of the Moslem community. The Toledo youth take pride in their religion and willingly cultivate religious activities on the bases of voluntary association.

Religious activities are associated with social progress in the minds of Toledo youth, but with traditional backwardness in the minds of Detroit youth. Toledo's sheikh is a respected social leader who enjoys high prestige in the community as well as in the larger society. Assistants to the leader of the mosque in Toledo are volunteers and are called "deacons," signifying the affection and regard which the community feels toward them. Thus the youth strive to attain such positions.

The vacuum of religious leadership in Detroit is found to be among the variables associated with the low degree of religiosity in this community. This vacuum is caused in several ways by the traditional attitudes of the first generation: a) Being more traditional and less assimilated, the community nurtures the sectarian conflict between Shi'ahs and Sunnis. This conflict weakens the position of a religious leader, for it is very difficult to reconcile this traditional sectarian dispute which, in fact, represents the struggle for social leadership. b) The traditional attitude of the first generation links Islam with Arabism and thus a non-Arab religious leader, however pious and learned, is not accepted in the Detroit community as fully as he is in Toledo. To the traditionalistic Detroit community, Islam connotes Arab nationalism more than religion, while it works the opposite way in the assimilated Toledo community.

It is clear now that the two communities display two different dimensions: Toledo's is the religious dimension while Detroit's is nationalistic. The latter dimension has weakened Detroit's degree of assimilation while the former was found to be associated with assimilation.

No doubt the different attitudes of the communities toward intermarriage have affected the over-all position of each on the scale of assimilation. Detroit, with its rigid attitude, has lost many Moslems who could have added to its degree of assimilation had they not been rejected and consequently individually absorbed into the American culture. Toledo's acceptance of such marriages has added an element which stimulated further assimilation.

The different sizes of both communities is another relevant variable. The Toledo community is much smaller and was thus more rapidly assimilated. The Detroit community is older than Toledo, but in this case smaller size had stronger assimilation powers than greater length of time.

Role of Women and the Family

Moslem women, even of the first generation, have played an active role in the social and religious affairs of both communities. Economically, they joined the labor force in business as well as in the factory, besides raising children and taking care of the home. In community affairs they are very active. The women take the lion's share of the work in raising funds for religious and national causes. While they are still conservative in Detroit, the women in Toledo have broken some firm traditions by attending prayers at the mosque.

The social status of Moslem women is becoming increasingly equalitarian in the family as well as in the community. In fact, the wife in Toledo dominates the family. The family structure is very cohesive and contributes to lessening the rate of juvenile delinquency in both communities. Also, there is a sense of community responsibility which puts a limit on the individual social and personal activities. Whenever a person misbehaves and commits any immoral conduct, he is first admonished by the community, and if he does not change, he is punished by banishment.

Religion and Assimilation

Both communities have achieved a high degree of assimilation despite the recency of their arrival in America. The absence of any physical or color traits to distinguish them from the American majority has helped in this respect. The English language and the American food are the only things which seriously bothered the first-generation immigrants. Pork is taboo in Islam as in Judaism. The strongest religious habit still maintained by the Moslems in America is the abstinence from pork: 88 per cent never eat pork at home. Only half of the remaining 12 per cent eat it often at home. This 6 per cent are those of the third generation who are married to Americans. Observing the requirement of fasting during the month of Ramadan is the weakest religious element: 61 per cent in Detroit do not fast at all, as against 45 per cent in Toledo. In both communities, 41 per cent of the first generation do not fast, against 57 and 66 per cent, respectively, in the second and third generations.

The high degree of religiosity in Toledo indicates its strong family structure. In fact, there is less conflict between generations in Toledo than in Detroit. This is the result of the narrow gap between Toledo's first and second generations on the continuum of assimilation. The second generation in Detroit complains of the traditional patriarchal attitudes of the first generation at home as well as in business. The members of the first generation in Detroit tend to exploit their children in business. Not only do they underpay them but they also watch over their spending habits. The business conflict arises also from the generations' differences in ways of merchandizing. The first-generation members are oriented toward maximum profit on each sale, while the members of the second generation are oriented toward sale in volume with less profit per sale. The wife in Detroit very often takes her husband's side against the children and this outrages the second-generation members who feel no family support.

The outlook of the Detroit first-generation members over the future of their offspring is one of disappointment, as if they were lost, while in Toledo it is one of appreciation for the way their children grow up in America.

In general, the members of both communities find life more satisfying in America than in the old country. They have gained wealth and prestige and have enjoyed full political freedom. The weaker religious activities are what the Detroit community members worry about. This problem is solved in Toledo by adjusting religion to the new environment.

Appendix

CONSTITUTION OF THE FEDERATION OF ISLAMIC ASSOCIATIONS IN THE UNITED STATES AND CANADA

Proclamation

We, the members of the Moslem Community of America, following the Koranic injunction, "Hold fast, all of you Moslems, to the rope of God and do not disperse," resolve to combine our endeavor the purposes hereinafter set forth do hereby proclaim the formation of the Federation of Islamic Associations in the United States and Canada.

Preamble

Every human being according to Islam is born pure by (fitrah) and bears within himself a Trust to know God and worship Him. In the pursuit of this ultimate end, the foremost obligations of the Moslem in this world are the acquisition of Knowledge and Experience. His guides in this inescapable endeavor are the Quran and the Sunnah revealed as an act of Mercy to assist man in the fulfillment of his Ends. A devoted Moslem constantly strives, through the careful nurturing of his soul and his body, to transform his whole personality and his attitudes to higher and higher levels of being, whereby his knowledge and deeds naturally reflect the highest spiritual, moral, intellectual, and social ideals of mankind.

Moslems, wherever they are and in whatever age they live, are individually and collectively responsible to learn, exercise, and spread the ideals of Islam, such as the dignity and supreme worth of every human being, brotherhood, and love among all mankind, and the absolute equality of every person before God. Their mere professing of the principles of Islam is the lowest degree of being a good Moslem.

As an expression of their obligations and services in the path of God, the Moslems in the United States and Canada shall organize themselves under the present constitution to promote and teach the spirit, ethics, philosophy, and culture of Islam among themselves and their children. They shall through this organization establish close contacts with all parts of the Moslem world and participate in the modern renaissance of Islam.

They shall try, through publications and otherwise, to expound the teaching of Islam and clarify its ideals and spirit. In this endeavor they shall try to point out the common grounds, beliefs, and common ends which other religions share with Islam.

In this age of international strife and unrest, they should draw on the spiritual, moral, and intellectual wealth of the Moslem civilization and contribute their proper share in the establishment of world peace.

The Moslem communities in the United States and Canada should organize themselves into Local Associations to translate the above objectives within their communities. These local organizations should, besides the teaching and observance of the principles of Islam, administer to the religious needs of the members of their community. They should also provide media for the religious, intellectual, and social needs of their members, and tender them with moral, legal, and financial comfort.

ARTICLE I
Name

The name of this organization shall be the Federation of Islamic Associations in the United States and Canada.

ARTICLE II
Place

The Federation of Islamic Associations in the United States and Canada shall be located in America or Canada.

ARTICLE III
Membership of the Federation and their obligations

I. All Moslems who are members of affiliated Local Associations or Moslems admitted to the Federation by the Board of Directors will be qualified for the general membership of the Federation.

II. Their obligations shall be as follows:

A. Each member shall endeavor to further the objectives of the Federation.

B. He shall pay promptly all dues.
C. He shall conduct himself in a way that his behavior will never adversely affect the Federation.
D. He will cheerfully fulfill any tasks assigned to him by his Local Association or the Board of Directors.
E. He will aid other members in the performance or fulfillment of their duties and goals.

ARTICLE IV
Organization

The Federation of Islamic Associations in America shall be composed of:

A. General Assembly
B. Board of Directors
C. Local Associations

I. General Assembly
 A. Membership
  1. Only members of the Federation of Islamic Associations in the United States and Canada acting through the annual convention shall constitute the membership of the General Assembly.
 B. Jurisdiction and Duties
  1. The General Assembly is the supreme body of the Federation.
  2. It elects the officers of the Federation.
  3. It selects a city for the next convention from those proposed by the member Associations.
  4. It has the power to amend the Constitution.
  5. It fixes the annual dues of the members.

II. Board of Directors
 A. Membership
  1. The membership of the Board of Directors shall be composed of:
   a. The duly elected representative of each affiliated Local Association.
   b. The duly elected members of the Executive Committees of the Federation.
   c. The Director, or his representative, of the Islamic Center, Washington, D.C.
 B. Jurisdiction and Duties
  1. The Board of Directors acting through its duly elected officers shall be the legal cooperated body of the Federation

with powers resting in it, under the Articles of the Constitution.

Its jurisdiction and duties shall be as follows:

a. To formulate laws to be voted upon by the General Assembly and to guide the locals in the attainment of the objectives of the Federation.
b. To recommend to the General Assembly future members to the Board of Directors.
c. To perpetuate the organization and plan for its expansion.
d. To plan for the annual convention.
e. To publish any journals, pamphlets, or releases necessary to further the purpose of the Federation.
f. To act as a supervisory body, with the capacity to advise the Executive Committees as well as other standing committees.
g. To appoint the working committees.
h. To register authorize the starting of a new Local Association.
i. Whenever members of the Executive Committee fail to execute their duties as required by the Articles of the Constitution, the Board of Directors shall try to correct such failure, and may, when the situation demands, assume the functions assigned to the Executive Committee.
j. The Board of Directors shall meet at least twice a year, during the convention, and six months later.

III. Local Associations

A. Origination

1. Any Moslem association may petition the Board of Directors for a charter.
2. Existing associations may be invited by the President of the Federation to join subject to the approval of the Board of Directors.

B. Powers and Duties

1. They shall hold meetings and engage in activities which contribute to the ends of the organization.
2. They shall require the attendance of the local members at the local association meetings.
3. They shall observe the religious holidays and participate in the preparation for such activities considered within the objectives of the organization.
4. They shall submit reports through their Director to the Board of Directors concerning the activities and conditions of their Association.

5. They shall follow the Constitution of the Federation and adopt by-laws to meet their local conditions, provided, they are in accord with the Constitution of the Federation.
6. The Local Associations are bound by the resolutions taken at the General Assembly and in their executions of these resolutions, they are bound to carry the instructions of the Board of Directors and the Executive Committee.
7. They shall fix and collect dues for the support of their Association.
8. They shall elect a representative to the Board of Directors.
9. They shall pay the fixed dues per member to the Treasurer of the Federation.
10. Each Local Association shall elect its own officers. The elected officers will be immediately registered with the Board of Directors and the Executive Committee.

ARTICLE V

Executive Committee of the Federation

I. Membership

A. Members of the Executive Committee shall be the duly elected officers of the Federation at the annual convention.

II. Qualifications

A. Must be a member of the Federation for at least one year.
B. All officers shall be at least 21 years of age.
C. The Board of Directors may recommend to the General Assembly that an officer should not be reelected.

III. Election of Officers

A. Officers shall be elected last day before the end of the convention by means of secret ballot in simple majority vote.
B. They shall be installed at the close of the convention at which they are elected.

IV. Jurisdiction and Duties

A. The Executive Committee is authorized to:

1. Transact business of the organization be it regular or special.
2. Make necessary expenditures from the Treasury of the Federation.
3. Require necessary information from any Local Association regarding its conditions.
4. Issue injunctions preventing Local Associations from activities inimical to the welfare of the organization specifically, and Islam as a whole.

5. Issue charters to petitioners who received three-fourths the vote of the Board of Directors.
6. Meet at least four times a year at the request of the President or upon the written request of three members of the Executive Committee.

ARTICLE VI

Officers of the Federation

Officers of the Federation of Islamic Associations in America shall be:

A. President
B. Vice-President (3)
C. Secretary (2)
D. Treasurer

I. President

A. Duties

1. To call and preside over meetings of the Executive Committee.
2. To represent the organization in outside activities.
3. To sign together with the Treasurer all expenditure bills.
4. To enforce the Constitution and to call the attention of any member whenever necessary.
5. To report on the activities of the organization to the convention.
6. To coordinate the work of all committees, and coordinate their efforts.
7. He is ex-officio member of every committee subject to his own discretion.
8. He is to call and preside over the meetings of the Board of Directors.

II. Vice-President

A. Duties

1. To replace the President in his absence.
2. He shall be in charge of the organization of Local Associations. The three Vice-Presidents shall divide among themselves this duty according to geographic regions.

III. Secretary

A. First Secretary—Duties

1. Shall keep minutes of the meeting of the Executive Committee.

2. Shall keep members of the Executive Committee informed of important current developments in the Federation.
3. Shall prepare the agenda of all meetings of the Executive Committee in advance.
4. Shall keep all records and correspondence with the organization.
5. Be in charge of preparing copies of resolutions adopted.

B. Second Secretary—Duties

1. Shall keep all minutes of the meeting of the Board of Directors and the business sessions of the conventions.
2. Shall keep a list of all members, their addresses, etc.
3. Shall act as liaison between the Board of Directors and Local Associations.
4. Prepare a tabulation of active members at the annual convention.
5. Shall handle the correspondence of the organization with Locals and unaffiliated.

IV. Treasurer

A. To keep the revenue books.
B. To co-sign checks with the President.
C. To prepare the financial report to be submitted to the General Assembly and circulated to all of its members, to be submitted to the Board of Directors when it calls for it.
D. To serve as a member of the Financial Committee.

ARTICLE VII

Committees

The following committees are necessary for the fulfillment of the objectives of the Federation.

A. Religious Committee.
B. Cultural Committee.
C. Public Relations-Publication Committee.
D. Inter-Moslem Cooperation Committee.
E. Social Activities Committee.
F. Mutual Assistance; Scholarship Committee.
G. Financial Committee.

II. The duties and powers of each shall be defined in the by-laws of the Constitution.

III. Other committees shall be formed whenever the situation calls for them.

ARTICLE VIII

Voting

I. Voting age shall be 18 years of age.

II. A quorum shall be by simple majority of members attending any business meeting.

III. Only present members at the Election Session may be elected to office.

ARTICLE IX

Conventions

Members of the Federation and all Moslems are invited to an annual convention to meet at a place decided upon at the previous convention based upon the invitations of the Local Association. The time of the convention is to be set by the Host Association, provided it meets the approval of the Board of Directors.

ARTICLE X

Amendments to the Constitution

The Constitution may be amended by two-thirds vote of the General Assembly.

AMENDMENTS TO THE CONSTITUTION

Adopted July 23, 1955

1. Article IV:
Organization—The General Assembly is the Supreme Body of the Federation, which delegates its authority to the Board of Directors as soon as it is constitutionally formed.
2. Article IV:
Board of Directors (II) a.—The duly elected representatives of each affiliated local association, the executive committee shall assign the number of the representatives of the local groups according to the proportion of legal membership of the Federation.
3. Article IV:
Board of Directors (II) b.—General Assembly elects one-third of the Board of Directors. The geographical distribution of the Board of Directors shall be observed. The Board of Directors has the right to invite a limited number of deserving active Moslems to its membership.
k. The term of office of each member of the Board of Directors is one year.

Bibliography

Books

ABBOTT, GRACE. *The Immigrant and the Community.* New York: The Century Co., 1917.

ACKOFF, RUSSELL LINCOLN. *The Design of Social Research.* Chicago: University of Chicago Press, 1953.

ADAMIC, LOUIS. *A Nation of Nations.* New York: Harper, 1945.

———. *What is Your Name?* New York: Harper, 1942.

ALIHAN, MILLA AISSA. *Social Ecology.* New York: Columbia University Press, 1938.

AL KASHIF AL-GHITA, M. *Asl al-Shi'ah Wa-Usuluha.* (In Arabic.) Beirut: Maktabat al-'irfan, N.J.

AMMAR, HAMED. *Growing up in an Egyptian Village.* London: Routledge, 1954.

AUDAT, YACAUB. *Al-Natiqun bil-dad Li Amirika al-Ganubiyya.* (In Arabic.) Beirut: Dar Rihani, 1956.

BARNES, HARRY ELMER, and OREEN M. RUEDI. *The American Way of Life.* New York: Prentice-Hall, Inc., 1950.

BARON, SALO WITTMAYER. *Modern Nationalism and Religion.* New York: Harper, 1947.

———. *A Social and Religious History of the Jews.* New York: Columbia University Press, 1952-1958. Vols. I-VIII.

BARRON, MILTON L. *People Who Intermarry.* Syracuse: Syracuse University Press, 1946.

BENEDICT, RUTH. *Patterns of Culture.* New York: The New American Library, August 1956.

BENNETT, JOHN W., and MELVIN M. TUMIN. *Social Life; Structure and Function.* New York: Alfred A. Knopf, 3rd ed., 1952.

BERGER, MORROE. *Bureaucracy and Society in Modern Egypt.* Princeton, N.J.: Princeton University Press, 1957.

BEWS, JOHN WILLIAMS. *Human Ecology.* London: Oxford University Press, 1935.

BLISS, FREDERICK JONES. *The Religions of Modern Syria and Palestine.* Edinburgh: T. and T. Clark, 1912.

BLUMER, HERBERT. *An Appraisal of Thomas and Znaniecki's "The Polish Peasant."* New York: Social Science Research Council, 1939.

———. *Critiques of Research in the Social Sciences.* New York: Social Science Research Council, 1939.

BOGARDUS, E. S. *Essays in Social Values.* Los Angeles: University of Southern California Press, 1944.

——— (ed.). *Essentials of Americanization.* Los Angeles: University of Southern California Press, 1920.

———. *Immigration and Race Attitudes.* New York: D. C. Heath and Company, 1928.

———. *Introduction to Social Research.* New York: Suttonhouse, Ltd., 1936.

———. *The Mexican in the United States.* Los Angeles: University of Southern California Press, 1934.

BRIM, ORVILLE G., JR. *Sociology and the Field of Education.* New York: Russell Sage Foundation, 1958.

BROOM, LEONARD, and SELZNICK, PHILIP. *Sociology.* New York: Row, Peterson and Company, 1958.

BRUCKBERGER, R. L. *Image of America.* Translated from the French by C. G. PAULDING and VIRGILIA PETERSON. New York: The Viking Press, 1959.

CARPENTER, NILES. *Immigrants and their Children.* Washington, D.C.: Government Printing Office, 1927.

The Catholic Encyclopedia. New York: Robert Appleton Co., 1907-1914, S. V., "Trinity, The Blessed," Vol. 15, pp. 47-57; and "God," Vol. 6, pp. 608-621.

CHAPIN, FRANCIS STUART. *Cultural Change.* New York: The Century Co., 1928.

CHASE, STUART. *The Proper Study of Mankind.* New York: Harper, 1956.

CHILD, IRVIN LONG. *Italian or American.* London: Oxford University Press, 1943.

CLARK, ELMER T. *The Small Sects in America.* New York: Abingdon-Cokesbury Press, 1949.

CLINARD, MARSHALL B. *Sociology of Deviant Behavior.* New York: Rinehart and Co., Inc., 1957.

DAVIS, KINGSLEY. *Human Society.* New York: Macmillan, 1949.

———, HARRY C. BREDEMEIER, and MARION J. LEVY, JR. *Modern American Society.* New York: Rinehart and Co., 1948.

DAVIS, PHILIP (ed.). *Immigration and Americanization.* New York: Ginn and Co., 1920.

DEAN, VERA MICHELES. *The Nature of the Non-Western World.* New York: The New American Library, 1957.

DICE, LEE RAYMOND. *Man's Nature and Nature's Man; the Ecology of Human Communities.* Ann Arbor: University of Michigan Press, 1955.

DODD, STUART CARTER. *Dimensions of Society.* New York: The Macmillan Co., 1942.

DUCASSE, C. J. *A Philosophical Scrutiny of Religion.* New York: Ronald Press Co., 1953.

DUNN, L. C., and TH. DOBZHANSKY. *Heredity, Race and Society*. The New American Library, 1952.

DURKHEIM, EMILE. *The Elementary Forms of the Religious Life*. Translated from the French by JOSEPH WARD SWAIN. New York: The Macmillan Company, 1915.

EISENSTADT, SHMUEL NOAH. *Absorption of Immigrants in Israel*. London: Routledge and Kegan Paul, Ltd., 1954.

ELMER, MANUEL CONRAD. *The Sociology of the Family*. New York: Ginn and Co., 1945.

———. *Social Surveys of Urban Communities*. Menasha, Wis.: George Banta Publishing Co., 1914.

ERICKSEN, E. *Introduction to Human Ecology*. Los Angeles: University of Southern California Press, 1949.

EVANS-PRITCHARD, EDWARD E. *Social Anthropology*. London: Cohen and West, 1951.

———. *Kinship and Marriage among the Nuer*. Oxford: Clarendon Press, 1951.

EVANS-PRITCHARD, E. E., *et al. The Institutions of Primitive Society*. Oxford: Basil Blackwell, 1954.

FESTINGER, LEON, and DANIEL KATZ. *Research Methods in the Behavioral Sciences*. New York: Dryden Press, 1953.

FISHER, RONALD AYLMER. *Statistical Methods for Research Workers*. London: Oliver and Boyd, 1925.

FISHER, SYDNEY N. (ed.). *Social Forces in the Middle East*. Ithaca, N.Y.: Cornell University Press, 1955.

FREUND, JOHN E. *Modern Elementary Statistics*. Englewood Cliffs, N.J.: Prentice-Hall, Inc., 1956.

FROMM, ERICH. *Psychoanalysis and Religion*. New Haven: Yale University Press, 1950.

FRUCHTER, BENJAMIN. *Introduction to Factor Analysis*. New York: D. Van Nostrand Company, Inc., 1954.

GARRISON, W. E. *The March of Faith*. New York: Harper, 1933.

GERTH, H. H., and C. WRIGHT MILLS (eds. and trans.). *From Max Weber*. New York: Galaxy Books, 1958.

GIBB, H. A. R. *Islamic Society and the West*. London: Oxford University Press, 1950.

———. *Modern Trends in Islam*. Chicago: The University of Chicago Press, 1947.

———. *Mohammedanism*. New York: The New American Library, 1955.

GINSBERG, MORRIS. *Reason and Unreason in Society*. London: Longmans, Green and Co., Ltd., 1948.

GITTLER, J. B. *Social Dynamics*. New York: McGraw-Hill, 1952.

———, *et al. Understanding Minority Groups*. New York: Wiley, 1956.

GOODE, WILLIAM J., and PAUL K. HATT. *Methods in Social Research*. New York: McGraw-Hill Book Company, Inc., 1952.

GUTTMAN, LOUIS, *et al. Measurement and Prediction*. Princeton, N.J.: Princeton University Press, 1950.

HANSEN, M. L. *The Immigrant in American History*. Cambridge: Harvard University Press, 1940.

HAWLEY, AMOS HENRY. *Human Ecology*. New York: Ronald Press Co., 1950.

HERBERG, W. *Protestant, Catholic, Jew*. Garden City, N.Y.: Doubleday, 1955.

HITTI, PHILIP K. *The Syrians in America*. New York: George H. Doran Co., 1924.

HOEBEL, E. ADAMSON. *Man in the Primitive World*. New York: McGraw-Hill Book Co., Inc., 1949.

HOMANS, GEORGE C. *The Human Group*. New York: Harcourt, Brace and Co., 1950.

HOSELITZ, B. F., *et al. The Progress of Underdeveloped Areas*. Chicago: University of Chicago Press, 1952.

HOULT, THOMAS FORD. *The Sociology of Religion*. New York: The Dryden Press, 1958.

HOURANI, A. H. *Minorities in the Arab World*. London: Oxford University Press, 1947.

———. *Syria and Lebanon*. London: Oxford University Press, 1946.

HUXLEY, JULIAN. *Religion without Revelation*. New York: Mentor Books, 1958.

JAHODA, M., and R. CHRISTIE. *Authoritarian Personality Critique*. Glencoe, Ill.: The Free Press, 1954.

KAHN, ROBERT L., and CHARLES F. CANNELL. *The Dynamics of Interviewing*. New York: Wiley, 1957.

KALLAN, HORACE MEYER. *Individualism; an American Way of Life*. New York: Liveright, 1933.

———. *Education Versus Indoctrination in the Schools*. Chicago: The University of Chicago Press, 1934.

———. *Why Religion*. New York: Boni and Liveright, 1927.

———. *Zionism and World Politics*. London: Heinemann, 1921.

KATZ, DANIEL, and R. L. SCHANCK. *Social Psychology*. New York: Wiley, 1938.

KROEBER, ALFRED L. *Anthropology Today*. Chicago: The University of Chicago Press, 1953.

LAZARON, MORRIS S. *Olive Trees in Storm*. New York: American Friends of the Middle East, Inc., 1955.

LEMERT, EDWIN M. *Social Pathology*. New York: McGraw-Hill Book Co., Inc., 1951.

LERNER, DANIEL. *The Passing of Traditional Society*. Glencoe, Ill.: The Free Press, 1958.

LERNER, MAX. *America as a Civilization.* New York: Simon and Schuster, 1957.

LEVY, MARION J., JR. *The Structure of Society.* Princeton, N.J.: Princeton University Press, 1952.

LEVY, REUBEN. *The Social Structure of Islam.* Cambridge: The University Press, 1957.

LINTON, RALPH. *The Study of Man; An Introduction.* New York: D. Appleton-Century Co., 1936.

LUBELL, SAMUEL. *The Future of American Politics.* New York: Harper, 1952.

LYND, ROBERT S., and HELEN M. LYND. *Middletown in Transition.* New York: Harcourt, 1937.

MACIVER, R. M., and CHARLES H. PAGE. *Society.* New York: Rinehart and Company, Inc., 1957.

MADGE, JOHN. *The Tools of Social Science.* New York: Longmans, Green and Co., 1953.

MALINOWSKI, BRONISLAW. *The Dynamics of Culture Change,* ed. PHYLLIS M. KABERRY. New Haven: Yale University Press, 1945.

———. *Magic, Science and Religion.* Garden City, N.Y.: Doubleday, 1954.

MALINOWSKI, B., *et al. Culture, the Diffusion Controversy.* New York: W. W. Norton and Co., 1927.

MEAD, MARGARET. *Cultural Patterns and Technical Change.* New York: The New American Library, 1955.

———. *Male and Female.* New York: The New American Library, 1955.

———. *Sex and Temperament.* New York: The New American Library, 1955.

MERTON, ROBERT KING. *Mass Persuasion.* New York: Harper, 1946.

———. *Social Theory and Social Structure.* Glencoe, Ill.: The Free Press, 1949.

MEARS, ELIOT GRINNELL. *Greece Today.* Stanford: Stanford University Press, 1929.

MILLER, DANIEL R., and GUY E. SWANSON. *The Changing American Parent: A Study in the Detroit Area.* New York: John Wiley and Sons, Inc., 1958.

MOORE, WILBERT E. *Economy and Society.* New York: Doubleday and Co., Inc., 1955.

———. *Industrial Relations and the Social Order.* New York: The Macmillan Co., 1951.

MYRDAL, GUNNAR. *An American Dilemma.* New York: Harper, 1944.

NOTTINGHAM, ELIZABETH K. *Religion and Society.* New York: Doubleday and Co., Inc., 1954.

PARK, ROBERT EZRA. *Human Communities.* Glencoe, Ill.: The Free Press, 1952.

———. *The Problems of Cultural Differences.* New York, 1931.

PARSONS, TALCOTT. *The Social System.* Glencoe, Ill.: The Free Press, 1952.

———. *The Structure of Social Action.* Glencoe, Ill.: The Free Press, 1949.

PARTEN, MILDRED. *Surveys, Polls, and Samples.* New York: Harper, 1950.

PAYNE, STANLEY L. *The Art of Asking Questions.* Princeton, N.J.: Princeton University Press, 1951.

PETERS, CHARLES C., and WALTER R. VAN VOORHIS. *Statistical Procedures and their Bases.* New York: McGraw-Hill Book Co., Inc., 1940.

PRATT, JAMES BISSETT. *The Religious Consciousness.* New York: The Macmillan Company, 1951.

Quran

RADER, MELVIN. *Ethics and Society.* New York: Henry Holt and Company, 1952.

REDFIELD, ROBERT. *The Little Community.* Uppsala: Almquist, 1955.

———. *Peasant Society and Culture: An Anthropological Approach to Civilization.* Chicago: University of Chicago Press, 1956.

RIESMAN, DAVID, *et al. The Lonely Crowd.* New Haven: Yale University Press, 1950.

ROSE, ARNOLD MARSHALL. *America Divided.* New York: A. A. Knopf, 1948.

———. *The Institutions of Advanced Societies.* Minneapolis: University of Minnesota Press, 1958.

ROSENTHAL, HARRIET C. *Intermarriage of Jews and Gentiles: A Study in Cultural Conflict and Acculturation.* Chicago: The University of Chicago Press, 1922.

SAENGER, GERHART. *The Social Psychology of Prejudice.* New York: Harper, 1953.

SAPIR, EDWARD. *Language.* New York: Harcourt, Brace and Co., 1949.

SCHERMERHORN, RICHARD ALONZO. *These Our People.* Boston: D. C. Heath, 1949.

SIDDIQI, MOHAMMED M. *Women in Islam.* Lahore: The Institute of Islamic Culture, 1952.

SIMPSON, GEORGE EATON, and J. MILTON YINGER. *Racial and Cultural Minorities.* New York: Harper, 1953.

SMITH, HUSTON. *The Religions of Man.* New York: The New American Library, 1959.

SMITH, WILFRED CANTWELL. *Islam in Modern History.* Princeton, N.J.: Princeton University Press, 1957.

SPENCER, HERBERT. *Descriptive Sociology.* New York: D. Appleton and Co., 1881.

SPERRY, WILLARD L. *Religion in America.* Cambridge, Mass.: Harvard University Press, 1946.

STANLEY, WILLIAM O. *Education and Social Integration.* New York: Columbia University Press, 1953.

STEPHAN, FREDERICK F., and PHILIP J. MCCARTHY. *Sampling Opinions.* New York: Wiley, 1958.

SUTHERLAND, EDWIN H. *Principles of Criminology.* New York: J. B. Lippincott Company, 1955.

TAFT, DONALD REED. *Human Migration.* New York: Ronald Press Co., 1936.

TAFT, DONALD REED, and RICHARD ROBBINS. *International Migration.* New York: Ronald Press Co., 1955.

TAWNEY, R. H. *Religion and the Rise of Capitalism.* New York: The New American Library, November 1958.

THOMAS, WILLIAM ISAAC, and FLORJAN ZNANIECKI. *The Polish Peasants in Europe and America.* 2 vols. New York: A. A. Knopf, 1927.

TIMASHEFF, NICHOLAS S. *Sociological Theory.* New York: Random House, 1957.

TORGERSON, WARREN STANLEY. *Theory and Methods of Scaling.* New York: Wiley, 1958.

TUMIN, MELVIN M. *Desegregation.* Princeton, N.J.: Princeton University Press, 1958.

UTLEY, FREDA. *Will the Middle East Go West?* Chicago: Henry Regnery Co., 1957.

VIDICH, ARTHUR J., and JOSEPH BENSMAN. *Small Town in Mass Society.* Princeton, N.J.: Princeton University Press, 1958.

WARNER, WILLIAM LLOYD. *American Life.* Chicago: The University of Chicago Press, 1953.

WARNER, WILLIAM LLOYD, and LEO SROLE. *The Social System of American Ethnic Groups.* New Haven: Yale University Press, 1945.

———. *Structure of American Life.* Edinburgh: University Press, 1952.

WARNER, WILLIAM LLOYD, MARCHIAL MEEKER and KENNETH EELLS. *Social Class in America.* Gloucester, Mass.: Peter Smith, 1957.

WASHBURNE, NORMAN F. *Interpreting Social Change in America.* Garden City, N.Y.: Doubleday, 1954.

WEBER, MAX. *The Protestant Ethic and the Spirit of Capitalism,* tr. by TALCOTT PARSONS. New York: C. Scribner's Sons, 1950.

WILLIAMS, ROBIN M., JR. *American Society.* New York: Alfred A. Knopf, 1952.

WIRTH, LOUIS. *The Ghetto.* Chicago: University of Chicago Press, 1956.

———. "The Problems of Minority Groups," in R. LINTON (ed.), *The*

Science of Man in the World Crisis. New York: Columbia University Press, 1945.

WIRTH, LOUIS, *et al. Community Life and Social Policy*. Chicago: Chicago University Press, 1956.

YINGER, JOHN MILTON. *Religion in the Struggle for Power*. Durham, N.C.: Duke University Press, 1946.

———. *Religion, Society, and the Individual*. New York: Macmillan, 1957.

YOUNG, DONALD RAMSEY. *American Minority Peoples*. New York: Harper, 1932.

Component Parts of Books

BARRON, MILTON L. "Research on Intermarriage," in MILTON L. BARRON (ed.), *American Minorities*. New York: Alfred A. Knopf, 1958. Pp. 450-58.

BERGER, MORROE. "Americans from the Arab World," in JAMES KRITZECK and R. BAYLY WINDER (eds.), *The World of Islam*. New York: St. Martin's Press, 1959. Pp. 351-372.

DAVIS, ALLISON. "Acculturation in Schools," in MILTON L. BARRON (ed.), *American Minorities*. New York: Alfred A. Knopf, 1958. Pp. 446-49.

DAVIS, KINGSLEY. "Romantic Love and Courtship," in DAVIS, BREDEMEIER and LEVY (eds.), *Modern American Society*. New York: Rinehart and Co., Inc., 1949. Pp. 587-92.

GLAZER, NATHAN. "Ethnic Groups in America: From National Culture to Ideology," in M. BERGER, T. ABEL, and C. H. PAGE (eds.), *Freedom and Control in Modern Society*. New York: D. Van Nostrand Co., 1954. Pp. 158-76.

GLOCK, CHARLES Y. "The Sociology of Religion," in ROBERT K. MERTON, LEONARD BROOM and LEONARD S. COTTRELL, JR. (eds.), *Sociology Today*. New York: Basic Books, Inc., 1959. Pp. 153-77.

HANSEN, MARCUS LEE. "Immigration: A Field for Research," in MILTON L. BARRON (ed.), *American Minorities*. New York: Alfred A. Knopf, 1958. Pp. 262-74.

HOURANI, ALBERT. "Race and Related Ideas in the Near East," in ANDREW W. LIND (ed.), *Race Relations in World Perspective*. Honolulu: University of Hawaii Press, 1955. Pp. 116-144.

MURPHY, GARDNER. "The Internalization of Social Controls," in MORROE BERGER, THEODORE ABEL and CHARLES H. PAGE (eds.), *Freedom and Control in Modern Society*. New York: D. Van Nostrand Co., Inc., 1954. Pp. 3-17.

SALEM, ELIE. "Problems of Arab Political Behavior," in PHILIP W. THAYER (ed.), *Tensions in the Middle East*. Baltimore, Md.: The Johns Hopkins Press, 1958. Pp. 68-80.

SILCOX, CLARIS EDWIN, and GALEN M. FISHER. "The Social Significance of Religious Differences," in MILTON L. BARRON (ed.), *American Minorities.* New York: Alfred A. Knopf, 1958. Pp. 52-68.

SIMPSON, GEORGE E., and J. MILTON YINGER. "The Sociology of Race and Ethnic Relations," in MERTON, BROOM, and COTTRELL (eds.), *Sociology Today.* New York: Basic Books, Inc., 1959. Pp. 376-99.

SIMSAR, MEHMED A. "Muslims in the United States, in LEFFERTS A. LOETSCHER (ed.), *Twentieth Century Encyclopedia of Religious Knowledge.* Grand Rapids, Michigan: Baker Book House, 1955. Vol. 11, p. 768.

SMITH, WILLIAM CARLSON. "The Process of Assimilation," in MILTON L. BARRON (ed.), *American Minorities.* New York: Alfred A. Knopf, 1958. Pp. 429-33.

Articles

BERGER, MORROE. "Social and Political Change in the Moslem-Arab World," *World Politics,* Vol. X, No. 4, July 1958, pp. 629-38.

BRADEN, CHARLES S. "Islam in America," *The International Review of Missions,* Vol. XLVIII, No. 191, July, 1959, pp. 309-17.

CRAIG, A. J. M. "Egyptian Students," *The Middle East Journal,* Vol. 7, No. 3, 1953, pp. 293-99.

DODD, STUART C. "Standards for Surveying Agencies," *The Public Opinion Quarterly,* Spring, 1947, pp. 115-30.

DOOB, L. W. "An Introduction to the Psychology of Acculturation," *Journal of Social Psychology* (Worcester, Mass., No. 45, 1957). Pp. 143-60.

FORD, ROBERT N. "A Rapid Scoring Procedure for Scaling Attitude Questions," *Public Opinion Quarterly,* Fall 1950, pp. 507-32.

GLASER, DANIEL. "Dynamics of Ethnic Identification," *American Sociological Review,* Vol. 23, No. 1, February, 1958, pp. 31-40.

GOLDBERG, MILTON M. "Acculturation of the Marginal Man Theory," *American Sociological Review,* Vol. VI, No. 1, February, 1941, pp. 52-58.

GOODMAN, LEO A. "Ecological Regression and Behavior of Individuals," *American Sociological Review,* Vol. 18, No. 6, December, 1953, pp. 663-64.

GUIDI, I., "Abyssinia," *Encyclopaedia of Islam,* Vol. 1, pp. 119-21.

HOUGHTON, LOUISE SEYMOUR. "Syrians in the United States," *The Survey,* Vol. XXVI (August 5, 1911), pp. 650-58.

ISSAWI, CHARLES, and DABEZIES, CARLOS. "Population Movements and Population Pressure in Jordan, Lebanon, and Syria," *The Milbank Memorial Fund Quarterly,* Vol. XXIX, October, 1951, pp. 385-403.

JENKINS, W. L. "An Improved Method for Tetrachoric r," *Psychometrika,* Vol. 20, No. 3, September, 1955, pp. 253-58.

MAKDISI, NADIM. "The Moslems of America," *The Christian Century* (August 26, 1959), pp. 969-71.

AL-MAQDISSI, NADIM. "The Muslims of America," *The Islamic Review* (England: Woking, June, 1955), pp. 28-32.

MURDOCK, GEORGE P. "Ethnocentrism," *Encyclopaedia of the Social Sciences,* Vol. V, pp. 612-14.

PARK, ROBERT E. "Human Migration and the Marginal Man," *The American Journal of Sociology,* Vol. XXXIII, No. 6, May, 1928, pp. 881-93.

PATAI, RAPHAEL. "The Middle East as a Culture Area," *The Middle East Journal,* Vol. 6, No. 1, Winter, 1952, pp. 1-21.

PROTHRO, E. TERRY, and LEVON MELIKIAN. "The California Public Opinion Scale in an Authoritarian Culture," *The Public Opinion Quarterly,* Vol. XVII, No. 3, Fall, 1953, pp. 353-62.

REDFIELD, ROBERT, RALPH LINTON and MELVILLE J. HERSKOVITS. "Memorandum for the Study of Acculturation," *American Anthropologist,* Vol. 38, No. 1, January-March, 1936, pp. 149-52.

RENTER, E. B. "Amalgamation," *Encyclopaedia of the Social Sciences,* Vol. II, pp. 16-17.

RICHARDSON, ALAN. "Some Psycho-Social Aspects of British Emigration to Australia," *The British Journal of Sociology,* Vol. X, No. 4, December 1959, pp. 327-37.

SAGI, PHILIP C. "A Statistical Test for the Significance of a Coefficient of Reproducibility," *Psychometrika,* Vol. 24, No. 1, March, 1959, pp. 19-27.

SIMPSON, FRANK T. "The Moorish Science Temple and its 'Koran'," *The Moslem World* (January, 1947), Vol. XXXVII, No. 1, pp. 56-61.

SMITH, WILLIAM CARLSON. "Changing Personality Traits of Second Generation Orientals in America," *The American Journal of Sociology,* Vol. XXXIII, No. 6, May 1928, pp. 922-29.

AL-TAHIR, ABDUL JALIL. "Isolation, Marginality and Assimilation of the Arab Communities in Chicago to the American Culture," *Bulletin of the College of Arts and Sciences, Baghdad,* June 1956, Vol. 1, pp. 54-65.

TANNOUS, AFIF I. "Acculturation of an Arab-Syrian Community in the Deep South," *American Sociological Review,* June 1943, pp. 264-71.

TUMIN, MELVIN M. "Rewards and Task-Orientations," *American Sociological Review,* Vol. 20, No. 4, August, 1955, pp. 419-23.

TUMIN, MELVIN, PAUL BARTON and BERNIE BURRUS. "Education, Prejudice and Discrimination," *American Sociological Review,* Vol. 23, No. 1, February, 1958, pp. 41-49.

TUMIN, MELVIN M., and ARNOLD S. FELDMAN. "Status, Perspective and Achievement," *American Sociological Review*, Vol. 21, No. 4, August, 1956, pp. 464-72.

TUMIN, MELVIN M. "Some Disfunctions of Institutional Imbalances," *Behavioral Science*, Vol. 1, No. 3, July, 1956, pp. 218-23.

———. "Some Unapplauded Consequences of Social Mobility in a Mass Society," *Social Forces*, Vol. 36, No. 1, October, 1957, pp. 32-37.

VOGT, EVON Z., and THOMAS F. O'DEA. "A Comparative Study of the Role of Values in Social Action in Two Southwestern Communities," *American Sociological Review*, Vol. 18, No. 6, December, 1953, pp. 645-53.

WIEBE, G. D. "Some Implications of Separating Opinions from Attitudes," *The Public Opinion Quarterly*, Vol. XVII, No. 3, Fall, 1953, pp. 328-52.

WOLF, C. UMHAU. "Muslims in the American Mid-West," *The Muslim World* (January, 1960), pp. 39-48.

YOUNG, JAMES N., and SELZ C. MAYS. "Manifest and Latent Participators in a Rural Community Action Program," *Social Forces*, Vol. 38, No. 2, December 1959, pp. 140-45.

Documents, Newspapers, and Unpublished Material

Constitution of the Islamic Federation.

Data Book, Toledo-Lucas County Plan Commission, Toledo, Ohio, July 1958.

The Economic Almanac. New York: Thomas Y. Cromwell Co., 1958.

The Federation of Islamic Associations in the United States and Canada. Washington, D.C.: The Islamic Center, N.J.

MAYER, ALBERT. *Ethnic Groups in Detroit: 1951.* Unpublished mimeograph, Wayne State University, Department of Sociology and Anthropology, June 1951.

News of the United Arab Republic (Washington, D.C., August 1959), Vol. 10, No. 8, p. 4.

Statistical Abstract of the United States, 1959 (U.S. Department of Commerce, Bureau of the Census, Washington, D.C.).

U. S. Bureau of the Census, *Religious Bodies: 1936.* Washington, D.C.: Government Printing Office, 1941), Vols. I-II.

U. S. Census of Population: 1950, *Special Report.* (Washington, D.C.: U. S. Government Printing Office, 1953), Vol. IV.

U. S. House of Representatives, *Abstracts of Reports of the Immigration Commission, with Conclusions and Recommendations and Views of the Minorities*, 61st Congress, 3rd Session, Senate Document No. 747, 2 vols. Washington, D.C.: Government Printing Office, 1911.

The World Almanac and Book of Facts for 1960. New York: New York World-Telegram, 1960, p. 715.

Yearbook of American Churches for 1960, ed. BENSON Y. LANDIS. New York: Round Table Press, Inc., 1959.

GRAVES, T. *The Muslim in America Stories*, printed in separate pamphlets by the U.S.I.A., 1959.

Al-Ahram, Cairo, Egypt, September 11, 1959.

The Detroit Free Press, Detroit, Michigan, September 22, 1953.

The Detroit News, Detroit, Michigan, October 16, 1953.

The New York Times, New York, N. Y., September 20, 1959.

Time, "Lebanon: Home Visit," August 3, 1959, pp. 26, 27.

Time, "*Races*: The Black Supremacists," August 10, 1959, pp. 24-25.

Toledo Blade, Toledo, Ohio, October 13, 1958, December 6, 1958, and March 12, 1959.

JIGGETTS, J. IDA. "A Study of the Absorption and Integration of the Yemenite Jew in the State of Israel." Unpublished doctoral dissertation, School of Education, New York University, 1957.

AL-TAHIR, ABDUL JALIL. "The Arab Community in the Chicago Area, a Comparative Study of the Christian-Syrians and the Muslim-Palestinians." Unpublished Ph.D. dissertation, University of Chicago, 1952.

Index